WE BUILT THE BRIDGE

WE BUILT THE BRIDGE

GRACE M. FALA, PHD

Illustrations by Dawn E. Hayes, EdD
Poetry by Frances Martha Barnes

ARCHWAY PUBLISHING

Archway Publishing books may be ordered through booksellers or by contacting:

Archway Publishing
1663 Liberty Drive
Bloomington, IN 47403
www.archwaypublishing.com
1 (888) 242-5904

Interior Image Credit: Dawn E. Hayes

ISBN: 978-1-4808-8283-6 (sc)
ISBN: 978-1-4808-8282-9 (e)

Library of Congress Control Number: 2019913861

Print information available on the last page.

Archway Publishing rev. date: 12/03/2019

In memory of Frances Barnes and Grace Straley.

In loving memory of and dedicated to Rose Iannetti Fala.

ACKNOWLEDGMENTS

My mother had a knack for sharing nuggets of wisdom, even in jest. As a brazen teenager, I often tested my mother's teachings. Her guidance then and now has been persuasive. She was steadfast with her encouragement to "trust God" and to value how "God works in mysterious ways." It might have taken years, but my mother's words have finally become realized.

I understand how God can be conceived broadly to include that which is divine; that which is holy; that which is good, beautiful, and wise; that which is true; that which is. For the purposes of this book, all a reader need do is to conceive God. You need not believe. A concept of God, as Descartes once suggested, is in and of itself a profound mystery.

Where does a thought of God come from? Who chooses what we think? How do we process awe?

Thoughts, according to Buddha, shape who you are. Ghandi once said that "if ever you want to change the world, change the way you think of it." Or perhaps, speak of it?

Discoveries and observations with nature, ancestors, family, and friends have planted in me thoughts of divinity. Some are also inherited from strangers. Even you have given me thoughts that inspire awareness of what Martin Buber highlights as our "thou." I have carried you and walked with you and have heard my heart humming because of you. I am grateful to you, the reader of these thoughts.

I also cherish those who gift their "thou" with me, who have nourished me throughout this journey. I am appreciative of each lesson and blessing shared. With love, I thank:

My ancestors, for their courage and dreams

My mother, for her laughter, mysticism, and prayers

My siblings, for their honest, trustworthy
and unconditional friendship

My nieces and nephews and their families,
for giving playfulness to purpose

Dawn's family, for their generosity and unending support

Everyone mentioned in this book, especially
Grace and Fran, for wings of inspiration

I'm also thankful to lessons learned from Rae Young
(Fran's sister); J. Bob Young (Rae's nephew); Fred and Myra
Morrow (Fran's nephew); Judy and Dennis Berman (Grace's
niece); Jack Troy (Grace and Fran's friend); John Schrock
(our friend); and George and Patty Knapp (read on).

In addition, we acknowledge:

Adora Smith, one of Franny's former students, who
maintained a lifelong friendship with her teacher
and assisted with helpful information

Donna Weimer and Juniata College, for nurturing a
community of beautiful people as colleagues and friends

Kirkridge Retreat Center, for sparking
colorful, soulful transformations

My students and retreatants, for an endless
supply of wisdom and creativity

GRACE M. FALA, PHD

My teachers, for their patience and values

Virginia Ramey Molenkott, for her words
of faith and her kiss of strength

Our friends and extended family members, who
have nourished us with love over the years

Our neighbors of Big Valley, who graciously
reached out to the strangers next door

We are also indebted to one of Grace and Fran's closest and beloved friends, Stephen Dunkle, for helping us authenticate our story. With much care, Stephen showed us the heart of Big Valley by introducing us to its people.

Shortly you will be reading about two amazing women who built the bridge that mortars our story together—Grace Straley and Frances Barnes. You will find their inspiration throughout the book. The poems that introduce each chapter are written by Frances Barnes. The cover design and all illustrations are by Dawn Hayes, with the exception of three that come from Grace Straley's artwork. Dawn and I proudly share their legacies and yield their creative (and perhaps divine) expressions with you.

I am most grateful to Dawn Hayes, who dares the adventure and lives this story with me. Her artful love has guided and steadied the words herein.

This story invites paradox and play. Thank you for giving your attention to it. We are honored that you have chosen to enter the story with a community of storytellers who will also read it. Your entrance will transform its organic constitution. When you exit, another story awaits and welcomes you.

Dawn and I welcome you to our story.

Amazing grace, how sweet the sound°...

CONTENTS

CHAPTER 1

PAUSE

The Chickadee's Song

"Chickadee, chickadee, chickadee, dee, dee,"
I know you're not singing for me, me, me.
You're singing most bravely,
For winter's still here.
Chickadee, chickadee, chickadee, dee, dee,
Why ever you're singing
I'll say it's for me.

Serenity envelops the chamber and settles in the belly of the rocks. A warm breath whispers among them. Otherwise silence stirs and is disturbed only by an occasional cock's crow in the distance. Each rock has been hand selected for its character and was mortared into a mural of find-and-seek images. In combinations, and with an imaginary eye, they form creatures. A lone wolf, for example, roams the upper right corner, while a creation turtle gnaws at the center nearby the breaching whale. A gravel hen and her peep hover by the arched, cinnamon door. Some rocks even look skeletal and spooky, but most configure into winged phenomena. Smaller than a garage yet bigger than a shed, this stone sanctuary is just large enough to fit the flutter of two angels.

While most of these boulders were born in the ground beneath them, the fossilized gemstones pressed into wings above the archway come from all around the world. Together they bend a local echo into global verse. Here, even bumblers keep perfect pitch. Erected to welcome and haunt whatever needs to awaken, perfect is, in fact, the pitch of this stone haven. Wrought iron ferns weighted into the arched door add forte to this crescendo. When you find yourself chirping like a chickadee, humming, chanting, or pontificating, you need not raise your voice to lift your spirit. You may never even need electricity again, especially if you think about how your Amish neighbors manage.

Whenever a blessing presents itself like a rock does, for example, pause to hold it close and listen. Breathe with it. Dream on it. Then fling it into a pond to affirm and return the favor. Not only will it change the vibration of the water (and arguably, the world), it changes you. You become more of your best self.

Numerous blessings of mine have been tossed into oceans, lakes, streams, and ponds, in various wishing wells and waterfalls too. Inevitably, those winged prayers that rippled across waterways years ago have landed me somehow here, in Big Valley. Now I sit inside these stone walls to reflect with bewilderment the potency of each pebble and to recall how what was once wished for unfolded.

Our journey started a few decades ago with a simple, pebbled prayer.

Dawn and I had looked for the ideal home for more than two years. We must have visited some seventy-five homes in a seventy-five-mile radius. We were, as usual, rather picky. She was particular about the aesthetic and structural integrity of the home, while I focused on the view. "Please give us a home with a view to savor," I pressed into the pebble before flying it across the sea. With impeccable timing, the northeastern stars must have heard my plea.

A gentle burst of spontaneity greeted us early on a Wednesday morning. Even though the growing season wouldn't be official for another month or so, we awoke to a spectacular spring day. We had waited a long winter for a moment as buoyant as this. I actually saw my first robin while drawing the curtains but couldn't wake Dawn fast enough to share my discovery. This is indeed the day! Today Dawn will come out to play with me. The rays were so magnetic it felt as if we had no choice.

Wednesdays are market days in Belleville. It didn't matter that Belleville was a forty-five-minute ride away. It didn't matter that we had no plans or needs to purchase anything; we had just gone shopping the previous night. The sun was what mattered. Being together mattered, as did the playfulness. So we hopped in the car and went for a drive.

On our way, we noticed how green life was becoming: the mountains, meadows, and pastures seemed to dress in drag to greet us. Dainty colors caught the morning light like feathered boas. You could actually catch spring bouncing off the air. Dawn and I had never really thought to look for a home in Big Valley. It appeared too far not because of distance, but because of difference.

An Amish community occupies most of the valley—farming families with horse and buggy, straw hats and bonnets, croplands and, most notably, dairy cows. Belleville, as the name suggests, is indeed a beautiful village. Life seems simple there but not easy. Most Amish families work day and night, in and out of each season. With kerosene lamps, occasional outhouses, and one-room schoolhouses, an Amish lifestyle can appear appealing, especially as the world dizzies itself with unnecessary distractions. Attractions with nature, on the other hand, can still the mind and steady the heart. After all, it might just be a butterfly that teaches us to remember precisely how to communicate.

A row of horse-drawn buggies was parked alongside the sale. Horses of all sizes, shapes, and colors stood sleepily, harnessed to mostly yellow and black, with a few white-top buggies. From the break of dawn to early afternoon every Wednesday, Amish farmers and English merchants set up their booths to sell their wares. According to most Amish and many of their non-Amish neighbors, Dawn and I are "English" even though I'm of Italian and Dawn is of German/Welsh descent. Anyone who is not Amish is usually categorized as English. Anyone who is not English is often referred to as Amish or Dutch unless you're neither English nor Amish based mostly on observations of complexion. Then you're likely generalized as a foreigner. For folks who need to confirm their own perceived differences of themselves and others, it's a category system that seems to work in its own stilted way.

Deep down I know how difference categorizes. I have been living a life of difference as a member of the queer community. Having challenged stifling adversity while coming out in the 1970s and 1980s, first to survive, then to thrive, I inherited a sensibility for justice and cultivated a deep appreciation for what people share in common. "Common" is the root of the word "communication" that, when leveraged, fosters compassion. That we trust the sun as it reaches for the trees. That we study the rain as it nourishes the fields. That we laugh when nature poses her paradoxes and dream while roaming the stars. We pray for our children's safety and mourn the growing pains. We enjoy song and food and yearn for love. We breathe the same air and hold dearly our last breath. Inside common ground, we take root, not because of who, how, or what life is, but because life is. That life is, is all that is. When sharing so much in common, differences sadly distance us. Belleville felt especially welcoming on this day though, despite our perceived differences.

From an urban or suburban perspective, the Belleville farmer's market can truly be a cultural phenomenon. The weather more than a clock determines if and when sellers set up or pack up their booths. By around 9:30 a.m., the auction for produce and homemade goods begins. And in the neighborhood of 1:00 p.m., livestock and poultry are sold. Farm time differs strangely from Wall Street time. Like riding a wooden horse on the carousel in Central Park, you can easily feel displaced, as if you had floated somewhere back into history. Dawn and I would know. We're authentic suburbanites with urban roots; it's written all over our faces. Nonetheless, we were easily charmed and taken in by valley peculiarities.

We were so pleased by the casual pace of the day that we decided to surrender our search for a new home and invest more in the house we lived in. Why bother to uproot now? What's the hurry? After almost two years of searching for a new home, we decided to let go of the obsession, to surrender our quest, and to settle comfortably in our abode in Boalsburg. Belleville left us feeling peaceful and resolved. It lured us into a complacency that reminded us that life was good.

CHAPTER 2

LISTEN

The Serious Salamander

Wouldn't it be dreadful
If a salamander-ay
Would sit upon a chair and stare
The livelong day?

For a salamander's serious,
As serious as can be.
I fear he'd stare a hole straight through
Wilmer and me.

For he never bats an eyelid,
And he never flicks his tail.
I studied one severely
When I poured him from my pail.

His spots were red from scarlet sage
That round our fish pond grows.
He slid beneath the water;
Then I watched him when he rose,
And he turned green as any grass:
It shook me to my toes.

As we set foot back in the doorway from our Belleville adventure, the phone rang. We almost tripped over ourselves to get it in time. Our Realtor felt certain she had found the perfect house and convinced us to act quickly, as this one would sell fast. Dutiful to her urgency, we scheduled an appointment for the very next day, after Dawn finished teaching. So much for letting go!

Thursday morning nabbed us back into routine. Dawn dashed off to school. I cleaned house, then went to meet my good friend Tracy for lunch. Tracy and I had waited a year for this meeting. Because of our busy work schedules, a meal together seemed impossible. But we persisted and managed to plan one. There's something about Tracy that gives life pause. A kind of kismet connects us, so few words are needed to express mutual affections. Plus, her smile is contagious.

I arrived early to the restaurant, carrying fresh flowers for my friend and promptly occupied a table out on the patio. Spring sensations leftover from yesterday lingered, so the place was packed. Outside was where I belonged; I had a hunch that Tracy would want to be there too.

The weather was clearly the headliner. Everybody wanted front and center, so much so that a line began to form. While sitting alone, noon could not approach more slowly at this bustling eatery. A hungry and hurried crowd groveled as the line grew. The more the patrons shuffled through, the more awkward I felt, especially when seated solo at a table for four. From a corner glance, I could catch their ravaging eyes condemning me for occupying such coveted space. To conceal the mounting guilt, I prominently marked my territory with a jacket, excused myself through the line, and sidled to my car for something to read. Making an escape granted momentary relief only. Out of a busted cardboard box of recyclables in the trunk, I grabbed a faded, dated newspaper. "This is barely big enough to hide behind," I mumbled before shuttling like a pinball back through the crowd.

The newspaper helped hide my red cheeks from the gawkers. I leafed through a few pages, uninterested in stale news. With one-foot tapping and the other headed for the door, I pretended not to appear agitated; agitation only summons more of what you don't want. Scavengers were already swooping down on me with their eyes. I wondered what happened to Tracy; this was highly unusual for her. Then, in a blink, something small caught my attention and stilled the shuffling; it was a boxed black-and-white photo, the size of a matchbox, printed near the fold of the paper. In it was a snapshot of a house to be sold at auction, nothing at all like the domiciles Dawn and I had been viewing. Nothing at all like the style, size, or location we had seen. This curious abode just so happened to be located in Belleville, of all places. As I began to read, a calm settled over me. I read it again and slowly again. Worry disappeared and scavengers turned into hummingbirds. Each soft word in the description flirted with me. I must have perused the ad a dozen times, attracted by its romantic lure. Cupid's arrow was dipped in a bowl of sweet persuasion that hour.

Each word echoed in the hollow of my soul. How could a simple ad in an old, crumpled newspaper be so sweet and enchanting? Suddenly my wait for Tracy was no longer a bother. I was no longer hungry for food or for anything; every appetite possible felt satiated. I had clearly found something. Or better yet, it had found me. I held onto it like string to a kite, feeling the wind between my fingers. I couldn't wait to tug it by telling Tracy all about it. Then, out of the blue, a frenzied waitstaff flagged me down as the lady with the long dark hair and sunhat. Tracy called and was running late and asked the management to notify me. In the day and age before cell phones, you sometimes just had to wait to process information. Another half hour had passed and since lunch break was winding down, I assumed that Tracy had to cancel.

If Tracy had kept her appointment for lunch, I would have never read that dated paper. Within an awkward, uncomfortable, potentially irritating missed meeting, an opportunity of a lifetime might have presented itself. Breath skipped through me with a purr. All I need do now is remain embodied, at least until Dawn gets home. I'll show Dawn my rare find and persuade her to drive back to Belleville.

Buoyant with excitement, I shared the news with Dawn the moment she walked into our home. Without missing a beat, she agreed. We would go immediately after honoring our appointment with the Realtor to visit a farmhouse for sale. Afterward, we were headstrong to follow our heartstrings. While the farmhouse was one of the nicer showings we had seen, it was missing the prerequisite views and simply did not resonate with us. We left knowing that soon we would snare an impulse—that felt more like divine intervention—and drive back to Belleville.

I was tickled to find Dawn also falling into the newspaper ad like a bee into nectar. She was stuck there too, somewhere between now and eternity. Following the newspaper directions like a treasure map, we headed back to Big Valley. Nothing could stop us.

CHAPTER 3

ATTEND

Young Skater

Was it I who went skating
alone, alone,
Dressed in plum velvet coat,
furred at knee,
wrist, and chin,
And a soft tam of fur with
a matching muff?
Was it I who went skating alone?
Was it I who saw the sun shine
on glittering lake,
Saw the slender, gold grasses
above the white snow,
Heard the crow cawing hoarsely
the treetops below?
Was it I who went skating alone?

Was it I who went whirling
and twirling along
On the meadow lake frozen?
Did I sing the song
Of the wind, and the lake,
and the grass, and the bird,
Of my lovely new garments?
Was it I who went skating alone?

The sun was setting by now in a soft drizzle. Just twenty-four hours ago, it had been over a year since we last visited Belleville. Now the spontaneity of yesterday teased us along the way as we approached this rural town, two days running. Acre by acre, sign after sign, we gathered the valley sweetness into our arms.

After dipping up and down long bends of valley terrain and ducking under canopies of trees and mountains, we finally arrived at the magical, gingerbread-like house. Wonderment took hold and I imagined us as children skipping gaily over the bridge while swinging picnic baskets high into the sky. We could find treasures along the way and toss them into each other's pouches for safekeeping. Then we would compose our postures like ballerinas before knocking on the big red door. Our archetypal grandparents will soon greet us with robust anticipation, no doubt. Receive and delight in the basket of treasures that, with a curtsy, we present.

Once reality reentered however, my childlike friend and I drove up the driveway at a crawl and with the trepidation of outsiders. Just as the ad foretold, it was lined with a stone bridge that curved around an open field. We were instantly and quietly charmed. Our intuitive attraction to the home was so overwhelming that it had become impossible to actually see it. We parked the car behind the taller blades of grass as if to hide and did what only we could do. We held our breaths.

Dawn jumped out first and sprinted toward a window. I was more reserved—worried that someone might still be at home. I couldn't believe her dare. Cowering around the car as if it were home base in a game of freeze tag, I studied Dawn's every move. She had the grace of a mist as it surrounds the early sun. Somehow, I knew we would be okay, but I didn't know it as well as she. I tend to move through time and space on blind faith, while Dawn moves faith blindly through time and space. I held myself back and watched her, amazed and lost—anxiously waiting to hear if the coast was clear.

With a confident wave, she beckoned me toward her. I would gladly receive an invitation of Dawn's, even in my dreams. With each precious day, she awakens what otherwise might be sleeping—beauty, goodness, and impish joy. "No... bod... y's... home," she bubbled like a goldfish, widening her mouth with each syllable to make it easier for me to decipher. Upon decoding the good news, I tiptoed cautiously yet hurriedly her way. She reached for my hand so we could peer through the window together giggling, in a blushing effort to muster bravery.

The sun had set by now. The silence of a mellow gloaming seemed to shelter us. I could feel nothing more than my own breath and Dawn's hand. Where are we? What is this magical place? Is this where the leprechauns hide, among tall trees and heavy stones? Covering the shadows with cupped hands around our eyes and with our noses peeled to the long windows, we found a simple and humble abode: wooden floors, brass lamp fixtures, an antique sewing machine, nonmatching sofa and chair. It struck us curious that there were no knickknacks. We desperately wanted a closer look. Once we trusted that nobody was home, we jiggled each door but couldn't get in—which was both a relief and a disappointment. Might we have entered if we could, despite laws and customs? Thank goodness the doors were locked; not having that temptation was indeed a relief!

Dawn remained quiet until we returned to the car. Knowing how picky she is, I wondered what was churning in that encyclopedic mind of hers as she latched the seat belt with extra emphasis. Once fastened in she said, "We'll just wait until Saturday for the open house." This statement alone from Dawn, who does not mince words, meant that she liked it, which in itself was rare. I knew I liked it, but that would be expected. Every home had enormous potential for me. I could easily imagine life unfolding under my feet, wherever they land. If a home had a view, I could be planted there; with a view, there's room to grow. I reminded her of the workshop I was scheduled to facilitate on Saturday at Shippensburg University. She wasn't fazed though; she had already mapped the day and devised travel plans: "Belleville is on the way. We'll stop here first, then head for the workshop."

Different qualities of our selves had surfaced as we entered and exited each prospective home. Some homes, for example, attracted the social self. Others enticed cultural or commercial pleasures. Some beckoned restoration, while others prompted adventure. This home did none of that. This home simply enchanted the soul like poetry.

We tried to drive home as though nothing happened. This helped keep emotions in check. Once we see the house by daylight and go indoors, we'll know more and perhaps feel better. After all, this house is up for auction. Houses sell "as is" at auctions. Anything goes; there are no guarantees.

I glanced over at Dawn as she drove us home. A delicate fusion of her deeper hues gradually dawned on me. Without realizing it, I had locked onto a small, colorful, getting-ready-to-leap frog painted on the barrette that cupped her golden hair. For a moment, I wished I were that frog. I'd sift through the gold as if it were Caribbean sand on a Sunday afternoon.

Dawn's warm, worry-free, and easy presence seemed to make her comfortable even in the most peculiar settings. With a rare and refined sense of diplomacy, she can negotiate a way in and out of any situation. Her entire body carries this sensibility—a calm assurance—with her wherever she goes. As her name suggests, just by being herself, she illuminates the moment. If we go hiking, she nourishes the forest. When climbing, she warms the mountain. When swimming, she makes the water sparkle, and when singing, she comforts. Being with her is a lot like being on perpetual vacation.

Sleeping was easy that night. The same silence that greeted us at the enchanted window stayed with us through the night. Something entered. Something remained. It was a passage of place at a place of passage, and it was Dawn. On Wednesday, she was my dear friend. By Saturday, she would become my soul mate.

I called my mother early the next day, excited to tell her about the newspaper ad, the miracle of Tracy missing lunch, and the cute home in Belleville. I tell my mother everything, especially since she knows fully how to harvest empathy. She makes dreams grow. Once conversation with Mama ended, I could actually sense the universe bend a little like a rainbow and with a quiver.

A well-fed heart made Friday a little easier to digest. After all, I would have to wait an entire day before seeing my new love again; that is, before the open house. Stars aligned with the sacred. I can still taste lips on the glass, on the window, from the leprechaun in the drizzle, on the golden hair.

CHAPTER 4

YIELD

Buzzy Bumble

"Sweets for me!
Sweets for me!"
Sang the pollen-laden,
Fuzzy, wuzzy
Bumble bee.

He sang a song of sun,
And of flowers in the sun;
he sang for all the bees
In the honey locust trees.

"Sweets for me!
Sweets for me!"
Sang the lacy-winged bee,
The big, black,
Busy, buzzy
Bumble bee.

Dawn and I awoke extra early on Saturday morning. Her name, as always, suited the moment. This was the day! The day of the rising! The open house! Without blinking, we packed props for my workshop, grabbed overnight bags, and selected outfits for dinner. It felt a little like Christmas day! We were toddlers again, wading through the immediate past, waiting to open the infinite present. With ticklish toes, we took off for Belleville for the third time in four days.

Testy and curious sprouts covered the fields, getting ready to burst into the warmth of yet another clear spring day. Unleashing our own adolescence would be easy on a day as capricious as this. Like monarch butterflies, we migrated naturally toward our destination and no longer needed the treasure map. It was crisp daylight now. We could easily see where the magnetic lure was drawing us.

A sloping stone bridge bordered the front driveway that upheld the majesty of a Stonehenge. We cantered up the driveway in our Volkswagen, as though riding bareback on a horse. Even though we were fifteen minutes early and the first to arrive at the open house, we were greeted with the full smiles of two strangers. A view of the heavens surrounded their reach. They introduced themselves as George and Patty Knapp, the current owners of the property. They were from Long Island, New York, and explained that they used the house for weekend retreats. Warmth and softness emanated from them, so much so, that we easily felt welcomed. Perhaps too easily though, we couldn't be sure. As two women we are often barraged with curious looks and awkward questions—for some reason not this day though, and not here.

Dawn and I approached the petite, white Cape Cod with slow, giant footsteps. Beyond the side door to the left stood a small forest of tall trees. From where we were standing, we could see oak, maple, locust, and hickory mostly, and a few ash. When we paused to look closely, the trees seemed to be saying something. Their message was as gentle as a sigh yet steady, like a hymn. Dawn reached out to touch them and shushed herself, as if to read their Braille with her fingertips. She glanced over to me with a face that told me she couldn't quite make out what they were saying. They rocked and chanted like monks in a monastery. I could feel them kissing my neck with their whispers. Not until Dawn released a whimper, did I finally hear. It was a faint message, but a clear one. "Look," they repeated and swayed. "Look."

There, where the branches pointed, was one of the most beautiful views I had ever laid eyes on! Beyond the side door to the right stretched lush green fields of high grasses, whimsical wildflowers, rolling hills of beige and golden cornstalks. Noticing our awe, "That's Big Valley," George proclaimed. The views were wrapped in a baby's blanket woven by the hands of God. I felt innocence lace through me. An angel fluttered, and my shoe came untied.

George then walked along the driveway to chat with visitors of the open house who arrived after us. It appeared as though all the other visitors parked along the street. For some reason, Dawn and I parked directly in front of the garage, as though we had special privileges. Patty escorted us into the kitchen and stood in front of the sink, which faced one of the wide windows we had peered into a few nights before. With a confidence nestled in wit and with warm eyes, she presented us with a simple vignette:

"Well, welcome to Stonebridge!" She paused to study us momentarily before continuing. "This home was built in the early sixties, 1962, I think, by two women who were both schoolteachers, Grace and Frances. One was an artist, the other a writer. Grace, the artist, drew the designs in this kitchen. Here, in this gold leaf cutting above the sink, you can see Grace and Frances working together in the gardens out back. Notice Grace holding a hand shovel and Frances holding a pen."

I glanced over at Dawn just as an excuse to do something with my eyes. I didn't want to appear as transfixed as I suddenly felt.

"They used to study organic gardening. As a matter of fact, their gardening books are still upstairs somewhere in the den. Grace used to work day and night in the arboretum out back. Folks around here still talk about that garden. It was apparently quite sophisticated and beautiful. We are fortunate to have a nice day today, wouldn't you say? Some of the spring flowers they planted have started to bloom."

Then Patty's voice carried some concern. She must have noticed that my jaw was dropping. I knocked Dawn with my elbow to jolt myself into believing that I wasn't alone.

"You can see the snowdrops and crocuses scattered among the ground cover." Patty peered momentarily out the window in the kitchen and then promptly returned to the conversation. "And if you look above the pocket door, you'll see a quotation in calligraphy that points to Franny's flare for poetry. It's derived from the book of Psalms."

We simultaneously lifted our heads to read the passage: "The lines have fallen unto me in pleasant places." Though neither of us knew the psalm, both of us nodded in understanding.

"Fran was apparently a whiz with words," Patty continued. "She occasionally wrote articles, mostly about nature, for the local newspaper. I'm pretty sure that a book of her poetry is also upstairs somewhere too." While pointing upward, Patty paused and looked around for more information. She wanted to make sure that she hadn't forgotten anything. "Oh, yes," she recalled. "And Frances loved to cook as well! Grace wanted Franny to have something nice to look at while Fran was cooking, so Grace painted this prayer in gold leaf above the stove."

Then with a more parental tone, Patty suggested we read the golden letters aloud together. She began and, even though the schoolteachers in us proudly accepted her directive, we did so with timidity. "Give us this day our daily bread and a good cook to prepare it, and we will eat it thankfully and with our guests we'll share it." Dawn was on her best behavior, which made me more antsy. When being proper, Dawn glides while I squirm. Actually, with added agitation, it's more of a squiggle.

Patty then indicated, "If you look carefully, you'll notice that Grace painted flowers and birds along the border of the prayer to complement the seasons of the year."

When her gaze stalled on Grace's artwork as if she had fallen into a daydream, Patty's smile emanated kindness. Catching herself, she returned and asked if we had any questions. We must have looked stunned. I fumbled and asked her to please repeat herself. Like a child would with a favorite nursery rhyme, I wanted to hear the beguiling story again and again. Reciting it verbatim would have been a cinch for me too. The story had landed in the palm of my hand like a firefly; it was indelibly aglow with each breath.

As reality slipped into illusion, I blurted, "Excuse me? Did you just say two women built this house? Two women, for real?"

"Yes," Patty replied. "Grace and Frances—one, an artist; the other, a writer."

"And both were teachers?" I confirmed.

"Yes, both were teachers. I think Frances taught high school language arts, while Grace taught elementary school."

"Well, what a coincidence! First of all, allow me to introduce myself. My name is Grace. I'd like to consider myself a writer someday. And this is Dawn who—by the way—is quite an artist. And we both happen to be schoolteachers." I waited expressively for some kind of response, though I don't know what exactly. Then I noticed a small statue of St. Francis on the kitchen windowsill, and by commenting that he was one of my favorite mystics, I hoped to ground myself in something familiar. It didn't work.

After hitting myself in the forehead with the balls of my fingers, I repeated and mumbled the query, "Two women?" I didn't know whether I was more mystified or stupefied. In disbelief, I looked to Dawn for clarity, but she was quiet and in an orbit of her own. Thoughts echoed in my mouth as I chattered nonsensically to no one. "Did you hear what she just said?" I wondered, half-dazed. "This house was built in the midsixties by two women. Both were schoolteachers, an artist and the other, a writer? And one was named Grace? What are the odds?"

Patty went on to describe features of the house while showing us the bedrooms. On occasion, she'd include nuggets of information on Grace and Fran. I felt attracted to her words and sipped on every syllable like a mirage in the desert.

The house was tastefully and thoughtfully designed. Its simple lines and curved corners, unique woodwork, and clever use of storage space added an air of sophistication to a humble homestead. After our tour of the rooms downstairs, Patty navigated us up the steps and into the den. Thank goodness she did. If she hadn't dropped anchor, we might have floated away. After a while though, she left us on our own and went to greet other onlookers of the open house.

Dawn and I were in the upstairs den, stuck inside a deep breath.

Since this was our first moment alone, I sought instant relief. A pinch would have helped when blurting, "Are you able to make sense of all of this? What do you make of it?" But Dawn was in a dream of her own and subdued. I hadn't noticed that she was crying. Her tears fell fast and free. She could not talk and had been engulfed within that space of no words. I reached for her with my eyes and walked closer, allowing the awe to unsteady us and to stop time.

A dreamy hour later, Dawn and I managed to land in the backyard. Patty had mentioned earlier that her husband would give us a tour of the old gardens. All we had to do was to find George. While searching for him, Dawn spotted something that looked familiar. With a tone of surprise, she drew my attention to a small, unassuming sign hanging from a dogwood tree at the edge of the driveway. "That's different! What does it say?" I quizzed while looking elsewhere. "It looks like a Jack Troy piece," Dawn said with intrigue. "No way. What does it say? It can't be Jack's. What leads you to say that?" I turned to find out for myself. "It's got to be Jack's," she insisted. "You can tell by the way it was fired." I inched over for a sharper look. Holding it like a photograph, Dawn explained how it was "a wood-fired stoneware plaque."

"Did Jack sign it?" I asked incredulously.

"Not that I can tell," Dawn replied with a raised eyebrow, detecting my disbelief. No way was it Jack's, I opined, not leaving well enough alone.

Jack Troy is a potter of international distinction who happens to work with me. The chances of it being Jack's were so slim that I dismissed Dawn's claim as mere conjecture. It was too much of a stretch for me to think that Jack had fired that plaque. How would he know Grace and Fran? He lives almost an hour away. While doubting the sign maker, I did not question its contents. With leaf imprints and stamped capital letters, the plaque read simply, "The Straley Barnes Arboretum." We soon found George and then sauntered with him into the remnants of Grace Straley and Frances Barnes's majestic gardens. Intrigue lingered and passions stirred. What was their story? What is it about this home? These gardens? This awakening? The prayers planted here?

George lit up like a Ferris wheel when he smiled. Greeting him a second time, however, we could sense some sadness in him too. We asked why he and Patty were selling since they both still seemed attached to the home. His pithy reply needed no explanation, "Family." Silence joined us as we strolled.

After a long pause, George added, "Our daughter is moving to northern New York with her husband. Their first child, our first grandchild, will be born soon. We'd like to be as close to them as possible, you see." Selling the house was apparently a heartbreaking decision for George. "The birth of a grandchild will make it all worthwhile, I'm sure!" he emphasized.

George paused to flip some of the sprawling thicket that covered a patch of delicate white flowers. He wanted to free them from vine congestion. Dawn and I could see how he nurtured a sweet sentimentality with each rescue. "It was Grace and Fran who planted them all. Patty and I just left the backyard alone and let it grow natural and wild. Look! There's a patch. See them? They fill the backyard on days like today! They're called snowdrops. They are the first of many of Grace and Franny's plantings to come up each spring. Next will be the glory-of-the-snow. They make the backyard an ocean of blue." His two new students had never seen or heard of such flowers and, while I was too imbued in the wondrous to learn anything factual, Dawn would surely take note.

With a calming voice, Dawn asked George to tell us more about Grace Straley and Frances Barnes. He was pleased to oblige. "Well, you know they built that bridge you drove over to get up here. Imagine two gals in their sixties building a stone bridge." His eyes glimmered with wonderment. "Grace actually studied hydraulic engineering, if you can believe that! She and Fran scrubbed each boulder, let them dry, and then they somehow set the boulders into place. I understand it took them a couple of summers to finish. Must have been while the house was being built, between nineteen sixty-two and sixty-four. We have the original blueprints in the house somewhere, if you want to see them."

"That's quite encouraging," I answered with hopefulness toward the future. Dawn glanced over at me as George summoned another onlooker and, with alert eyes, whispered, "Patience and Sarah. Grace and

Fran remind me of Patience and Sarah." I smiled back happily, connecting the dots. Written by Isabel Miller, *Patience and Sarah* is a fiction about the lives of two women who pioneered trails for warriors like Grace and Fran. Since they were obviously educated professional women, I also wondered if Grace and Fran shared a "Boston marriage" like those documented by Lillian Faderman in her classic book *Surpassing the Love of Men*. Starting in the late 1700s England through the early 1900s United States, women who were affluent and/or well-educated could choose to live in "romantic" relationships with other women. Their independence from men also encouraged participation in various social, cultural, and political causes. Some relationships were forged out of necessity. Others were formed among women who preferred the company of women to men. Either way or both, these trailblazers helped forge pathways of liberation for all women. While not all Boston marriages were romantic according to Faderman, many were.

Curiosity lifted my feet as I tiptoed around each of the flowers to avoid trampling them. With closeted nervousness, I wanted to impress George, knowing that sellers can be selective when choosing who wins at auction. Whenever I try to leave an impression, however, I'm bound to make a fool of myself. After the first few idiotic blunders, I returned to that peaceful silence for solace. I have since learned that impressions are already etched in the spaces between people. We only think we're making them when, in actuality, we simply stretch the ones already there.

The story of Grace and Frances kneaded tenderness into the air. Their lives helped to familiarize understandings of two women living together with common affinities. Such familiarity eases and warms our welcome today. Dawn and I extended our thanks to George and Patty. Even though I hardly knew them, even though we were among the "public" at an open house, I wanted to hug them before saying goodbye. I decided to embrace them with my eyes instead. A hug might have been inappropriate. Like being the only guest to park in the driveway, I couldn't be sure. But there was something I still needed to know, something that was keeping me from leaving.

"Curiously," I asked before parting, "How did you acquire this property? Did you know Grace and Frances?"

Patty was happy to share. "Yes, we knew them. They sold us this home before moving to Valley View, a retirement center in the heart of town. You probably passed it on your way here. We heard they were selling through friends of ours who own a bed and breakfast on Back Mountain Road, across the valley. We used to travel to the valley on weekends for retreats before Grace and Fran sold us this house. Apparently, we were the only ones that passed the interview!"

"The interview?" I questioned.

"Yeah, the way Grace and Fran sold this house was somewhat unconventional. With much scrutiny, mind you, they interviewed all potential buyers and selected the best fit. And that happened to be me and George, I guess!" she said jokingly to ensure that she did not sound boastful.

Smiling back, I then asked, "Do they still live at Valley View?"

"Well, Fran has passed on, I'm sad to say. She passed on a few years back. But Grace is still with us. Unfortunately, she has a bout of Alzheimer's. Some days are clearer than others, you understand." After a courteous pause, Patty went on to ask, "I'm curious. How did you hear about the open house, anyway?"

"We saw the ad in the *CDT*, our local newspaper," I replied.

"Really? We only ran the ad one day in that paper. We assumed people wouldn't want to come out this far," she added.

Amazingly, that same day's paper happened to be the exact one I rummaged out of a recycling box in my trunk, only because Tracy missed lunch.

With their rhetoric and thoughtful presentation, George and Patty knew how to honor the memories of Grace and Frances. Even though the only couple that passed Grace and Fran's test had owned this house for the past four years, they still considered its history when sharing it with the public. On some level, Dawn and I constituted this public. But, on another level, we sensed something happening that was very private and a little frightening too. Whatever the phenomenon was, it would carry us into new awareness of and respect for the mysterious. Mystery tends to make a home in the pits of stomachs. We knew we were home. We had no idea how on earth we got here, the first to arrive and the last to leave! Yet we knew precisely what drew us to Stonebridge—paradox and play.

We remained at Stonebridge for three hours, hoping to stay forever. Dawn and I thanked the Knapps once again and felt relieved that there was a second open house scheduled for the following Saturday. We assured them that we would be back. Every fiber of my being was suddenly focused on Grace. I had to meet her, to get closer to the weaver of all this wonder, to wallow in her stories and be woven repeatedly by her magic. It was just a matter of time before we'd meet.

CHAPTER 5

LEAP INTO THE PUSH

Forgive Me Now

Will you forgive me while the heart beats strong
And life flows free and vigorous each day,
Or will you hold your spite and grief prolong
Throughout the way?

Dear friend, let us be kind to each other;
The time grows old, and ills beset the road.

The lion's in the street, the owl's abroad,
The wolf howls blindly in the cold and dark.
Deny me not the spark
Of understanding.

Let me come in to warmth
and light and love,
Which cometh from above.

Dawn drove in slow motion down the driveway, catching every glimpse of the home from every angle possible. I wanted to leap freely and aimlessly into conversation. I like talking through everything, just to make sure that things are real. Dawn mulls through everything before talking. I use words to understand thoughts. She uses thoughts to understand words. I speak as a way of thinking; she thinks as a way of speaking. Words and thoughts—a chicken and egg dilemma! In any case, she needed absolute silence. I smiled from a deep-seated place of contentment and whispered, "Okay," to myself.

We crept past Valley View Retirement Community, where Grace was living. I waved to Grace with the wings of my imagination. Then, with the impetuosity of a teenager, I took advantage of the silence. There, in front of me, on the wide screen of my inner eyelids flickered Le Grande Dame's movie debut, featuring the pioneering lives of Grace and Franny. I started to recreate their gallantry. After teaching for thirty-some-odd years, Grace and Fran blended their talents to design the home of their dreams. Grace must have done the sketching while Frances, the conceiving. Grace might have been the strategist and Fran, the gatekeeper. Based on her skills as an artist, I pictured Grace's creative attention to detail. And Frances was probably wily with words, given her passion for poetry. One thing was evident—with bravery and moxie, Grace and Fran led parallel lives.

Imagine these two sixty-something-year-old women using pen and pencil, tongue-in-cheek, to wield the courage of warriors. Both would work interdependently to clean, lift, load, and place each stone into that bridge. It had to be a twosome from beginning to end. How did they handle the weight, the weather, and the wonder of it all? Ironically, common parlance would have pegged them merely as feeble spinsters. Yet, the common has never been the means or measure of the uncommon. Imagine Grace and Fran living life and love in their own extraordinary way, hauling heavy boulders to rest. Imagine their strength needed as two women, especially in the mid-twentieth century, to be free.

As Dawn and I gamboled with pride across the backbone of Grace and Fran's lives, we were reminded of a book of powerful essays edited by Cherrie Moraga and Gloria Anzaldua. Its title is telling: *This Bridge Called My Back*. A compilation of essays, this book validates many of the fundamental changes that stretch our tomorrow because of the blood, sweat, and tears of the pioneers who made that tomorrow possible.

Suffragists, civil rights activists, individuals with disabilities and persons of color, for instance, broke (and still break) their backs so that others could live and love freely. They built volumes of bridges for others to cross over. Much of our future continues to be carried and lifted by today's builders of freedom.

Because of their backbreaking efforts, that which Grace and Fran shouldered, is now, for me and Dawn, less like boulders and more like rocks. Hopefully through work of our own, the rocks we inherit will become pebbles for the next generation and erode eventually into sand. "Now that we know where Grace lives," I mused, "we can learn more about the bridge she and Fran built." With her stories, perhaps Grace will build once again and become our teacher.

Fortunately, the two-hour ride to Shippensburg gave the time needed to graze on our dreams. After features of their documentary lives played in my mind, I took out a trusty pencil and notepad and proceeded to strip our house in Boalsburg and clothe the new home in Belleville with our Boalsburg furnishings. Nothing could lull the awakening energy. Other than a ladder and a lamp, we wouldn't need a thing! With the exception of window dressings, every room in the Belleville beauty was fully furnished by the time we got to the workshop. In my mind's eye, everything fit perfectly.

Soon after arriving at Shippensburg, Dawn and I went out for dinner. We chose to enjoy a pricier than usual meal together; after all, in a presumptuous way, we had a lot to celebrate. Dawn had not so much as peeped about our shared experience at Stonebridge. I tried to steady myself from bouncing off the seat so I could broach the topic with a soft touch. After placing our orders, I asked with discretion, "Can we talk about it yet?" She smiled, looked sweetly at me, and affirmed, "Yes." Then she paused to complete her thought with conviction, "That's the one."

Could it be? Was I hearing things, or was that just an echo of my own thoughts? Honestly, it was all I really needed to hear. I sensed her readiness to leap with me. And, as expected, I had a lot of talk stored up. I immediately shared furnishing plans with her and delighted in the attention she gave the details. With pencil and napkin, Dawn proceeded to draw a floorplan of each room. "This area here could double as a library, and see, in that space," she pointed, "we can place the piano." She already had memorized every inch of the building as if she had lived there for generations. With stars on the horizon, we indulged each other's wild-eyed dreams. By the time dessert arrived, we were strategizing finances while pondering the impossible. Dawn knows clearly what she knows, and most times, I know nothing clearly. But now, the knowing was different, more like an apparition that no one else sees. Thank goodness for the balance that Dawn offered and for the dialectic tensions of apparent opposites. Perspective from anywhere at this time validated the absence of rationality. And when rational thought did surface, it only got in the way. Creativity was in the air, as was joy—two of the best tools for teachers to share.

Because of the interplay between the playful and the meaningful, the interactive and the reflective, attendees often refer to my workshops as retreats. I also prefer the term retreat to workshop. It more accurately describes what we mutually experience. Usually I prepare before facilitating retreats, but anything usual, however, was to be neither expected nor allowed, since hearing the story of Grace and Frances. "I'll have to wing it," I whispered to myself. It won't be the first time winging it, either. But this time, the wings were real; I could fly. The retreat was supposed to focus on communication and courage. And it did, but now it too turned magical! It too was a happening, a serendipity! Words sounded more like lyrics and work became play. Surely, goodness transpires when beauty emerges. With one story, I had fallen in love. With one interaction, I had become enchanted. In one breath, the miracle of Dawn had become a much bigger miracle—if that could even be possible. In the blink of an eye, Grace and Frances, the romancers of Stonebridge—had transcended themselves. The energy of breath and blink carried me through the creative retreat with the sweeping motions of a ballroom dancer. Everything flowed seamlessly, and never before had my evaluations been more positive!

By the end of the next day, my mother, Dawn's parents and grandparents, each of my six siblings, seven nieces and nephews, friends, and colleagues would learn of our unfolding mystery. A radio broadcast would have been easier! We already yearned for Stonebridge, which was only slightly difficult. Serendipity was becoming a friend that we could trust somehow, even though the house might, after all, end up with another bidder. We tried to contain our emotions, but to no avail. A leave of absence from the ordinary and a leap of faith into the extraordinary was all we needed. But it wasn't a leap entirely. It was more of a push. Besides, we'd rather have that infamous love that's lost than not to have loved at all. We would also rather have faith that's lost than not to have faith at all. Especially if being lost means being somewhere, or with someone, other than expected. If so, then lost was where we had to be. Among the playful possibilities, we fell strangely into love once again. We were being pushed specifically this direction.

Only two days had passed since Saturday. Dawn and I subdued the impulse to drive out after school each day to make sure the house was still there—to make sure it wasn't all a dream. We decided to wait until Wednesday. It would be midweek by then with only three days of waiting and three days more until the next open house. Next Saturday's open house was going to be a very special day anyway. Months ago, my mother and three sisters together had booked what we call "Sisters' Weekend."

Sisters' Weekends take place only once a year. We usually reserve it months in advance to accommodate everybody's busy lives. This particular one happened to be scheduled for the Saturday of the second open house. I couldn't believe the timing. They had already planned to meet at our home in Boalsburg, a four-hour drive for them. This was quite fortuitous, and added to the coincidental nature of the Stonebridge saga. Angels must have known ahead of time exactly what they were doing. Having members of my family see Stonebridge before auction would be necessary for me to feel fully secure before bidding on it. I would need their blessings and intuitions to make everything right. So I called my sisters and invited them to the open house, since they were going to be, amazingly, in the neighborhood anyway. To my delight, but not to my surprise, they graciously obliged. Now it was just a matter of time.

CHAPTER 6

STAY CURIOUS

I teach at Juniata College, a small, refined, liberal arts college located in central Pennsylvania. Preoccupied with new love, I felt compelled to share the percolating news of Stonebridge with friends and colleagues on campus. They were kind to caution me about the risks involved with real estate auctions and quick to remind me that Belleville was really far from Juniata. "Far" was the disturbing word. I had no idea of the distance, or if distance should even matter. But it suddenly did. Distance had become a stirring wake-up call to reality.

The wind in my sail had deflated just a little, but only briefly, until I called Dawn and explained what colleagues had said. Dawn assured me that she would check the computer for an exact time and mileage reading. She did. The drive between Belleville and Juniata College is exactly twenty-three miles and should take approximately thirty minutes. If accurate, I would be ten miles and fifteen minutes closer to Juniata from Belleville than from Boalsburg. Why, I wondered then, did it seem so far to everybody? It must be the cultural distance more than the actual location of Belleville. The name "Belleville" conjures up images of Amish families, horses and buggies, farmland, crops, livestock, manure, and hence, distance. For the local urban or suburban resident, Belleville is far because it is different—especially for two women to occupy the same home. Perceived (or misperceived) and imposed differences make it seem distant.

Dawn met me after school, and even though it had been only three days since our last visit, we drove to the *Straley Barnes Arboretum* in Belleville again. It felt like an eternity since we had last seen it. We longed for the private time to dream there. The Knapps weren't likely to be home in the middle of the week, so we brought a blanket, sat on the front yard, and picnicked there. Then with camaraderie, the sunset decided to join us for dinner.

After drinking in the views, we made the calculated drive to Juniata College. I needed to be convinced of the exact time and distance. Plus, getting a sense of place in a place that wasn't really making sense might be helpful. The drive was just as the computer predicted. In fact, we made it to Juniata in twenty-five minutes, slightly better than suggested. Sails were set in motion once again. My colleagues probably didn't realize how instrumental they were. They helped us find a much-needed boundary. They also gave us a realistic way to anticipate the competitive nature of auctions. Until then, I was convinced that angels would take care of everything and were in full control. I was merely along for the ride, learning to trust the wisdom of strangers, who may very well be angels in disguise anyway. So, with a newfound air of caution, Dawn and I started looking into the logistics of auctions.

When we weren't at school, we spent the rest of the week cleaning and preparing for our guests who arrived that Friday afternoon. It was refreshing to see Diane and Loretta, my older sisters, and Camille, my younger sister, together again. My mother, Rose, brings blessings with her wherever she goes. She looked especially beautiful in the surroundings of her four daughters. My mother's gentleness emboldens our lives and opens safe spaces for sharing. With her voice, touch, and laughter rooting us, we plant dreams inside conversations. When her "gals" come together like this, we also become children again—loud, ticklish, boisterous, and giddy, sensitive, and dreamy too.

My sisters immediately claimed their rooms, took control of the kitchen, and proudly displayed the homemade foods they brought—most made by my mother's hand. The counter was soon overflowing with lasagna, pizzelles, fig and lemon cookies, rice pudding, and biscotti. With revelry and rivalry, we still stretch the truth to seize credit for our mother's gifts. Each sister had speeches to present, stories to tell, and flea-market treasures to find. Already overwhelmed by the panoramic maze of their weekend plans, I grew sleepy and wanted to nap. But napping was out of the question. It would take too much time, especially when sisters could otherwise be talking. My mother, however, has an eternal sense of time; she dozed off within minutes of their arrival. She usually waits until the roost is secure and the laughter is rolling before nodding out. With prayerful intuition, she knows when to let go and precisely when to hold on.

With a robust and replenishing laughter, Rose gets and keeps us going mostly because she finds joy in whatever we say and do. She even giggles when her daughters tell her that she has a direct line to the heavens. People who know her know Rose as a holy person, gifted with a transcendent personality. She emanates what she cultivates—love, everywhere and in everyone. Having witnessed her faith in action, many have learned to trust her goodness fully, since her whole life has been a prayer unfolding. Such gentleness can only be inspirational. So naturally, her feedback on the house would carry a lot of weight.

Diane is the oldest of the seven siblings. She has had more years, more responsibilities, and more ways of negotiating than the rest of us. She also has a stand-up comedy routine that only those who know her would find funny. But to Diane those who know her represent the world and, therefore, the world must think she's funny. It's indeed hysterical. Even her former students from years ago remind Diane of how funny she once was and still is. Diane, an art teacher by trade, lives life and livelihood in the realm of family. If you're in, you're in for good no matter what, and there's nothing that Diane wouldn't do for or give to you.

Loretta, the middle of seven, (three older and three younger) can afford to be more afloat with her views. She has expensive taste and generous pockets. Buoyant is where she belongs. With a punster's sense of humor and the precision of a wordsmith, she stays uplifted. Wisely astute yet innocent Loretta frolics with the angels and keeps close watch over anything that even smells suspicious. This way, those she loves are shielded by her care and sheltered by her vigilance.

Cammy is the youngest sister, and the sixth of Rose's seven children. She's the natural and practical sibling, comfortably assertive with herself and her views. She provides us with an audience, especially when we find ourselves funny. Cammy digs her feet into wherever things grow. Her creativity helps her to bluster through life like a field of colorful wildflowers: delicate and dedicated, celebrating the day, sensitive to the seasons, yet determined to flourish.

Sisters spent the first night of our special weekend telling jokes and singing silly songs off-key into an amplified microphone. Each of us performed, karaoke style, on a makeshift stage. Here, in front of sisters, we could act like Broadway stars. Tomorrow, the jokers and crooners will spend the morning among the Amish, the "plain people," of Big Valley.

CHAPTER 7

WHAT WE'RE LOOKING FOR FINDS US

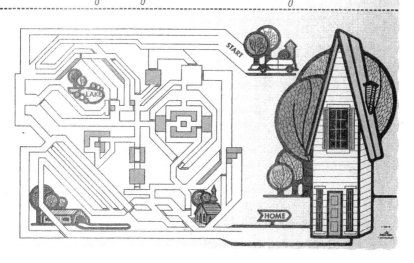

CROSSROAD PUZZLE
Find your way home thru this road maze...

This day would be the fifth visit to Belleville in ten days for Dawn and me. Before embarking, I asked my sisters—especially Diane—to be on their best behavior. I was trying to leave the Knapps with a positive impression again, still unsure of how they would regard two women as potential buyers. Diane rolled her eyes with a smile and mumbled, "What, you don't trust me?" I winked and let go, once again too excited to let any insecurity fester.

This time we were not the first but we were easily the largest group to arrive at the second open house. Dawn jumped out first to take pictures to send to her parents. Glad to see us, the Knapps waved us in but were busy showing the house to others. No worries. As if knighted by the rocks, I took immediate charge of the family tour. Our guests—along with everybody else we knew—had already heard the story of Grace and Frances. So my sisters' tour began with the presentation of Grace's artwork. Plus, it's only natural that we enter the kitchen first. After the initial show-and-tells, we walked from room to room, intuiting and studying ourselves in this special place. Then each of us walked her own path. My sisters were surprisingly unobtrusive. I couldn't help but wonder if something was wrong. My mother was also quiet, but that was to be expected.

I hadn't seen Dawn since arriving, so I set out to find her. Maybe she decided to stroll the gardens or to take pictures of the bridge? But she wasn't in the gardens. Nor was she on the bridge. After checking rooms downstairs, my curiosity led me upstairs to the den, where Frances used to write poetry. There she was, standing in the center of the room. Quiet tears again tumbled down her face. But she was not alone this time. My sister, Diane, stood motionless beside her. They were both crying. Each had touched something profound, or better yet, something profound had touched them. The sight of them arm-in-arm and awestruck was so awakening that I had to join in. Something was happening—something simple, deep, loving, and mysterious. The three of us held on to that which was holding us together. We took a deep breath to inhale the prayers of Grace and Frances and to exhale the majesty of this sacred site.

We spent a little over an hour at Stonebridge that day, but just as we were leaving, Diane—who is even more sensitive about leaving good impressions—was sorely trying to kiss up to the Knapps. She's worse at it than I! As the eldest, she believes she has the right to investigate thoroughly anything that might be of value to her younger siblings. "Umm, would you say this is a nice neighborhood? I mean, umm, how do you get snow off the driveway? Do the big trees ever get in the way? You know my sister's a professor. She teaches at a college. And the other ladies who lived here were teachers too?" As she rambled through her litany, the Knapps looked at each other quizzically, waiting for their turn to respond. I realized that she was just being Diane. She was doing what she does so well, leading the clan and protecting her kid sister. But I truly wanted to zip her shut and shuttle her out the door! Instead I blushed and hid under the heavy lids of my eyes. The trails that Diane blazes have made life easier for me and the rest of our family. No doubt that she has earned her rights to beauty and blunder. ("There but for the grace of you, go I.")

The excitement started to catch up to us and had worked up our appetites. Flustered and famished, we all remained quiet until we could enjoy something to eat. Peachey's Restaurant, just outside of Belleville, featured a Saturday brunch buffet and had plenty of available seats. As soon as we entered, it was plain to see that we were not your average local ladies. My sisters are suburbanites too—makeup, jewelry, pocketbooks, heels. These are out-of-town trappings and dead giveaways, though the gals weren't fazed in the least. They're rather natural at usurping the space they're in and at making themselves feel right at home. There's a tacit understanding our family shares—a kind of norm: Home is where the family is. It doesn't matter where we are. What matters is whom we're with. However, at this particular moment, I felt more like an outsider, not quite belonging anywhere. Given the circumstances and bizarre coincidences of late, my sense of self seemed to be unraveling.

A Mennonite woman wearing a pastel blue dress and white cotton apron took our order. She was one of a handful of women dressed in similar fashion who worked there. Her hair was in a bun, tucked under a sheer white bonnet. No makeup. No jewelry. No heels. No need. Her demeanor was warm and friendly, which was a relief. Awkward as it was, she might after all someday be a neighbor. After our eyes met and slight smiles exchanged, I didn't feel so much the stranger anymore.

As we waited for our meals, Dawn was fiddling around with the place mat under her elbow. She drew our attention to the design. It was a puzzle called, "Find your way home." You entered the maze at the upper left-hand corner of the mat. Then you'd navigate your way through the labyrinth until landing safely at home. "Home" was sketched in the lower right-hand corner of the mat. It happened to be a picture of a small white Cape Cod. Geographically—and serendipitously— Boalsburg is northwest of Belleville. If looking at a map, our journey to Belleville begins in the upper left-hand corner and weaves around to the lower right-hand corner of central Pennsylvania. A stretch? Maybe. Weird? You bet! But with everything else that was going on, it would have been more illogical to doubt than to believe.

Why not? With the realm of infinite possibilities opening lately, there was plenty of room for yet another coincidence! My sisters, amused by Dawn's discovery, chuckled that the moment had its own funny bone. But I was more anxious to hear about their every thought regarding the house and remained distracted. So I readied myself for their feedback, realizing that the wind beneath my sail might stir again.

Cammy spoke first. She came up with the game rules. "Let's go around the table, one by one."

"Yes, good idea!" I quickly responded. "You go first."

Diane and Loretta seemed nonplused by the plan, especially coming from a kid sister. Dawn and my mother sat back as though preparing for the long conversational ride.

"Let's let Diane go first," Cammy quipped. "After all, she is the oldest," placing full emphasis on the verb "is."

Diane was still unusually quiet. Was she okay? What's going on with her? "I don't mind going first. I don't mind going last," she jested.

She had become fastened to a meticulous probing of the spices in her sandwich. Diane has had lots of food allergies. She has to be careful. Meanwhile, Loretta returned to the menu to sort through dessert options. She wanted to make sure that everybody was well-fed and that our mother—who is diabetic—would enjoy a special Pennsylvania Dutch dessert. She was also scheming to pay the bill, like she often does. My sisters were unexpectedly subdued throughout the meal—still chewing on the experience of it all, perhaps? Either that or they needed more caffeine.

GRACE M. FALA, PHD

Nobody was in a hurry; nobody was in a fuss. Nobody even mentioned the house. This—in itself—was bizarre. It was—like everything else—most peculiar. We usually vie vehemently for the attention and jump into the first available conversational space. But this was neither the time nor place for anything usual. So the unusual occurred. My mother and sisters must have been mulling over their own enchantments. I decided simply to let go and to watch. Stillness settled. Instead of talking about it, we commented on the food and the service and wondered about the lives of the Pennsylvania Dutch.

With a tease, I inquired hesitantly, "Well, what did you think of the house?" They all agreed that "it was nice" and that they would "talk about it later." They "needed time to think on it." Once fed and fueled, we gathered our timidity and headed back to Boalsburg.

In the car, they could see that I was preoccupied. They did not intrude. I could see through the rearview mirror that, if a soul had emotions, their souls had been crying. Gratitude softens us and holds us together on a wave of empathy. I also let dry tears fall as we drove out of the valley. This was clearly a pivotal moment in my life. That they should be here with me during this time of emergence was profound. I felt a love for my sisters that surpassed any and every magical coincidence. This love was the greatest miracle of all—there was no coincidence about it! Look to the ordinary for the extraordinary. Look to the common for the exceptional. Look to the sibling beside you, the stranger within and without, for the divine.

CHAPTER 8

YOU ARE WHAT YOU WISH FOR

A Daisy Field

A daisy field is the freshest thing.
Awake on a dewy May morning
And they're dancing before the sun.

Soft petals white in a circle race
Around an enchanting, golden face
Thrust upward toward the sun.

At home in field, in town, in stall,
By manor house, by broken wall,
True aristocrat of flowers all
Is this day's eye, this daisy.

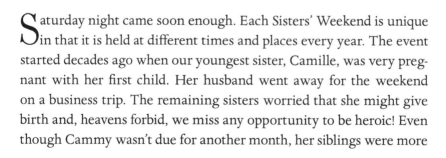

Saturday night came soon enough. Each Sisters' Weekend is unique in that it is held at different times and places every year. The event started decades ago when our youngest sister, Camille, was very pregnant with her first child. Her husband went away for the weekend on a business trip. The remaining sisters worried that she might give birth and, heavens forbid, we miss any opportunity to be heroic! Even though Cammy wasn't due for another month, her siblings were more than willing to stand guard just in case. Loretta suggested we pack overnight bags and head to her house to keep watch. All night long, we paced as though Cammy giving birth was more a probability and less a possibility. Stories, sentiments, and silliness kept us awake into the early hours of the morning. Just as her obstetrician predicted, it would be another month before Cammy actually would give birth to her son, Ryan. Nonetheless, the anticipation of Ryan's birth brought us together. Our pajama party was so renewing that Loretta made us promise to do it again at least once a year. Now sisters alone, with mom, leave their coops and kids once annually for some weekend fun.

Long ago, when we started, we found ourselves reliving two favorite memories from previous years. Both have since become mainstay customs of Sisters' Weekend, having withstood the test of time. One, I cannot tell. Telling would breach the confidence of sisters being silly. The other custom has more merit, thankfully. Each year, following our mother's lead, we make wishes. If we find a wishing well, we'll drop coins. If we're near a body of water, we'll skip stones. If we're under the canopy of stars, we'll twinkle-twinkle the little ones. If we're eating at a fancy restaurant, we'll salute the chef. If candles are handy, we blow out more wishes. Wherever there are pebbles, there are prayers.

Even though wish time was slowly approaching on Saturday night, the delay in hearing about the house had turned suspense into suspicion. I couldn't figure out why my sisters were talking about everything else but the house. Don't they know how much it means to me? Do we really need to unearth each ingredient in a delicious Italian wedding soup again? How many times do we have to compare, contrast, and contradict, well, anything? There must have been something about our visit today that confounded them. So before setting our wishes free, I approached my mother and each sister individually for feedback. I spotted Diane first. She happened to be in the dining room, setting the table for coffee and dessert. The oldest of Rosie's seven hesitated to find the right words but did not pause when placing napkins next to plates. With eyes reddening, she quivered:

"Do whatever you have to do to get that house. Beg, borrow, and steal if you have to. If you have to rob Peter to pay Paul, do it. If you have to go bankrupt, do it. Don't ever let anything get in the way of a dream come true. I'll do whatever I can to help." She repeated this message until all her tears had fallen. As her words trembled, the earth quaked a little beneath my feet too. I grabbed a few utensils and fumbled with her to finish setting the table.

Later, I spoke with Loretta, who was in the bathroom redecorating. It soon became apparent that she had studied Stonebridge much like an architect would. With a robust agility for words, she commented on how beautiful the views were and on how aesthetically pleasing the house was. She was most descriptive about the interior design, an area of specialty for her, and offered insights on wall colors, tiles, woodwork, and curtains. Such keen eyes for detail later led her to ask helpful questions. In her own sagacious way, she was protecting me. She wanted to make sure that I was clear in my own heart. With her encouragement, I talked through my feelings. Then she asked more pointedly, "Do you trust that you'll be safe there, Grace? You and Dawn? Two women in such a rural area? What is your gut feeling?"

Her blend of caution with compassion resonated. Beyond any dream, she wanted me safe and sound. "If you feel that you'll be safe there, then go for it, sis!" I also appreciated her alertness. We sat for a long while and talked. Then I went to find Camille.

Cammy was lounging on the sofa in the living room waiting for someone, anyone really, to rub her feet. "What do you think about the house?" With eyes squinting and nose snuggling into the pillow, she squeaked, "Grace Marie, will you rub my feet?" I sensed that she was trying to find words to say something hard in a gentle way. So I nervously began to rub her feet. "Cammy?" I asked with half my mouth closed.

Without opening her eyes, "You know, this house in Boalsburg is very nice, Gracie. It's in a great neighborhood, close to shops and schools. You and Dawn like it here. If things don't work out, you still have this house. It's a very nice house, you know; I mean this one here," she repeated. "Can you and Dawn afford to move? Put more pressure on the arch, will ya? I mean that place in Belleville might sell for a lot more than you think." I continued to press with a little more firmness. With a boisterous smile she continued, with eyelids down, to give specific foot-rubbing instructions.

Cammy was being practical and realistic. These are her fortes. And, like Loretta and Diane earlier, she was being protective. Not because she thought I'd be deprived the dream of a lifetime, not because I'd be unsafe. Cammy worried that we wouldn't win the auction, that the house would be too expensive for our budget. She imagined some wealthy tycoon scooping up the win. Indeed, it was possible. But I did not—could not—see that possibility, not for one moment. It was helpful that Cammy reminded me though. This way, in case we did lose, Cammy would be the first person I could call. She had the perspective I needed. She's like my mother that way.

"Yeah," I agreed. "If we win, great. If not, so be it." Cammy wanted me to prolong the massaging, but I was on a mission. The matriarch was next.

I had no trouble locating my mother. She has always been easy to find. While peeling broccoli rabe over a basin in the kitchen, she asked gently, "What did your sisters say, doll baby?" I gave her the full account and then asked what she thought. "Pray on it," she asserted confidently. "Whatever is God's will, be done. If it's meant to be, it will be." She concluded, as she usually does, with a melodic sound that has a lilt and an upbeat tempo, "Umm-beh! So be it!" She puckered her lips and puffed it into life. I caught the wind of that message with a hug and set sail again.

Just as we were beginning to fling wishes aimlessly into the living room like rose petals, Dawn joined in with a bounce in her step. Wishes are wondrously infinite and plentiful. All we need do is to breathe to set them free. So, after the first whirl, we pretended to toast ourselves to yet another round of wishes. It was indeed a full weekend. We ate a lot. Talked a lot. Laughed a lot. And dreamed.

CHAPTER 9

TRUST

Just Hibernate

Have you ever wished to creep in a hole
And curl up tight from the weather?
Have you ever longed to be a bear
And sleep forever and ever?
Cheer up, sweet lass, this mood will pass,
And you'll find your spirits rising,
When the sun shines gold and the wind in the grass
Brings spice scents warm and enticing.
Then your sleeping spirits by winter chilled,
Lying hidden deep as sap in the oak,
Awaken to loving kindness and hope
Buried beneath life's snow-white cloak.
So bend when the load is heavy,
Let the spirit be silent and gray,
For the soul has need of a resting place
As the heart must rest in its lifelong race:
We must wait for the lilac spray.

The next day, we faxed the terms of the auction to my oldest
brother, Herman, who is the humblest big-shot real estate lawyer

you'll ever meet in the city of Philadelphia. He chuckled at first at the offbeat legal customs of rural Pennsylvania. Not many properties are sold at auction in the City of Brotherly Love. Some terms needed to be spelled out and clarified. The basic terms, however, were clear: 10 percent down the night of the sale, to be paid in full within thirty days. By examining both process and procedure, Herman explained what to anticipate, what to allow, what not to allow, when to worry, and when not to worry. He provided the assistance of a muse, steadying us every step of the way, so we reported news concerning Stonebridge back to Herman almost daily. His presence throughout was, in sentimental ways, symbolic. Had he been alive and healthy, my father might have asked similar questions and offered similar advice. With a soothing confidence, Herman makes life easier for everyone in the family, especially during significant transitions like these. Like my mother, he has always been easy to find.

Only ten days had passed since I found that simple ad in the newspaper. Well, since the ad found me. It was a Thursday, the day after the weekly barn sale in Belleville. That same Thursday night, Dawn and I had driven to see the house for the first time. It was dusk by time we arrived, too dark to see the property fully. On Saturday, we attended the first open house. We spent the morning there, soaking up the story of Grace and Frances and sipping on the view. The following Saturday was Sisters' Weekend and the second open house.

Now, in less than a week, we would have to prepare ourselves—financially, legally, culturally, emotionally, and spiritually—for the bidding and for the possibility of losing the bid. The auction was scheduled for 6:00 p.m. the very next Friday, April 23. April 23 just so happens to be Dawn's birthday. Yet another coincidence, no doubt! Not to mention that her parents were planning a visit that day anyway to celebrate her birthday. Dawn was relieved that they would have a chance to study Stonebridge in person too, especially before the auction began. Like most members of my family, they also live nearby Philadelphia, a three-to-four-hour drive away. Apparently, the Tao was already set afloat between families long before the magical house ever appeared. Yes is the answer and nowadays the question too.

GRACE M. FALA, PHD

As the week unfolded, Dawn and I sorted through the attic treasures of our emotions. We rummaged. Dumped. Dusted. Polished. Discovered and inquired. Thursday eve, the night before the auction, was a bit haunting. Emotions peaked in an air of thin silence. That mysterious trust that kept us afloat also anchored us. We sat quietly, looked long at each other, and felt strange. What was ahead of us? Were we ready for this? Had the winds of fate already been set in motion? Did we have any control over what was about to happen?

Love, the language of the universe, was palpable, as was justice. Buying a home together was the closest and only representation at the time to symbolize (and perhaps sanctify) our commitment to love. It is the only "marriage" imaginable that either of us will likely experience. We need to be brave like Fran and Grace, especially if they wedded their lives the only way legally possible, through this property. Owning land together represented one huge step (and the only one available) toward the freedom to sanctify love. What might have been denied to them through exclusionary practices or rumored about them through stagnant customs would have been eroded in a small yet significant way through land ownership. Whirlwinds of misperceptions can drape weight around hearts with wings. Thank goodness that their wings were melded into the stone that bridged our path because without doubt, we were embarking on a mutual spiritual journey.

While gazing at Dawn and preoccupied with possibilities, I broke the sappy silence with a simple question, "What are you most afraid of?" Dawn's response was immediate and naked: "That we don't get it." Then she asked wearily in kind, "What are you most afraid of?" Her patience permitted me an unusual amount of response time before answering, "That we do get it." If we do, it would come with such profound purpose that for now is unpredictable and even unpreventable.

It was a relief to finally acknowledge the fear. We feared the power of this grand mystery while, at the same time, we somehow knew to trust it. That night we learned to respect and trust our fears.

CHAPTER 10

EMBODY THE PRAYERS
OF YOUR ANCESTORS

Rain Song

The rain on the roof
Above my head
Drips lightly down,
Drips lightly down.

The little drops whisper,
"It's time for bed.
Put on your gown,
Put on your gown.

The great drops rattle
And splash in glee.
They sing of spring,
They sing of spring.

The ginkgo roots
Are drinking free
Their leaves to bring,
Their leaves to bring

The rain clouds pass,
And the cool, pale moon
Goes riding by,
Goes riding by.

I hear from my window
A sure spring tune,
The wild goose cry,
The wild goose cry.

The mist is rising
Along the hill,
A ghostly thing,
A ghostly thing.

It will fall tomorrow
And flood the rill
To complete the ring,
To complete the ring.

When our sleepy eyes greeted the new day, Dawn was a year older. We woke on Friday, April 23, with scattered birthday wishes, auction jitters, oiled prayers, and shoulder shrugs for this "let's wing it" day. The auction was scheduled to begin at 6:00 p.m. Dawn's parents would meet us there at five. This would give them an opportunity to examine the house in person. Even though they had seen pictures, their personal experience was needed and necessary. It was now their time to bless Dawn's dreams. Whatever the outcome, we would surely celebrate Dawn's birthday with style by going out to her choice of restaurants afterward.

Dusk arrived early on the twenty-third. The sun set in soft drizzle once again. This mellow twilight had become a friend. Last time, at this hour, Dawn and I had been peering discreetly through windows, looking for fairy dust, thankful that nobody was home.

We had three cars with us that night. Dawn met her parents in

Harrisburg where she was attending a conference. Then they followed each other to the valley. I drove separately and was the first to arrive, forty-five minutes early. I parked alongside the stone bridge and appreciated the time alone to pause, reflect, and pray. I could hear the echo of my mother's words, "God's will be done." As the water gurgled under the bridge, I mused at the neighbor's cow. We were both mulling over things. Then I recalled the immigration of my grandparents whose language and culture were estranged in their new homeland. I thought of my grandmother's strength and courage and remembered my grandfather's gentleness. I longed for my father's intuition and blessing. Although all were long gone, I wanted them near that night, especially my grandmother. She would have been Fran's age. She would have used laughter to hold my hand and to lead the way.

When Dawn and her parents pulled up soon after, the trees that lined the driveway waved us all in. I kept a friendly distance, realizing this was their first visit. They needed a fresh experience. They walked along the gardens, into the garage, through the house, and back to us. They seemed okay with their first impression, but I really couldn't tell. Perhaps her parents had entered the zone of enchantment? I had to ask Dawn to decipher their body language for me. She told me she could tell that they liked it, but they were worried it might sell for too much. I couldn't tell how she knew this since they didn't utter a word, but she seemed quite sure of herself, so I trusted that she knew. They were apparently protecting Dawn with their own version of caution.

Dawn was comforted that they were there. This was a pivotal moment in her life too; their presence made a loving difference. I also relinquished some worries and relied on the shared wisdom of Dawn's parents. We agreed that Dawn should do the bidding since it was, after all, her birthday. All she would need is the wave of her finger, a nod of her head or targeted wink of an eye. No identification required. No numbers issued. No words spoken.

A crowd of around thirty people started to gather outside the garage. The sight of them made us panic a bit. Obviously, the more bidders, the higher the bids. Who were most of these wranglers anyway? Where are they from? How much money can their pockets possibly hold—enough to compromise our passage, to jeopardize our soon-to-be dream-come-true? Many must be locals; they're wearing dark flannels with mud-scuffed jeans, muck-scuffed boots, and distressed baseball caps. Half of them were Amish, and a handful must have been from out-of-town, like us. We out-of-towners were dressed more formally for what looked to be quite a casual and common event.

The auctioneer conducted a few sound checks on his pignose amp—the size of a shoebox—and then proceeded to describe attractive features of the house. The microphone squealed, and he began with, "What we have here folks is a real humdinger! It's a beautiful Cape Cod with an arboretum out back! It's got a stone patio, a foundation all ready for your barn, and some really nice trees here too!" Before we knew it, the bidding was underway. There were approximately twenty-five people clustered in a circle, sheltering the rain. Dawn and her parents and I stood beside the huge oak tree near the side door. At first, there were four curious onlookers bidding. After prices climbed, there were three. One nod of a head later, the competition narrowed down to two finalists.

Initially, Dawn looked clammy and exasperated, like she was trying really hard to keep her act together. She was determined not to fold at the knees, but she stood closest to the big tree just in case. The calculated wave of her buying hand was slow and heavy. She almost had to use one hand to help lift the other. With every bid, every raised hand, the price increased by five thousand dollars. Her fingers were frozen in the position of a puppet with its mouth open. Once she saw and studied our leading opponent, however, she perked up and started betting like a precocious schoolgirl who raises her hand with cool confidence in each answer.

We were bidding against another woman who stood alone, with her back to us—well, with her back to everybody. She stood with one leg forward and hand on hip directly in front of the auctioneer. There was aloneness to our opponent's bidding behavior that even enveloped her eyes. She did not look at anybody, as though she was the only one there. Or as though she was the only one that mattered. She was tall, thin, sharp and—in our imaginations—wicked. She suddenly became a cartoon enemy with hidden powers for jinxing. Even the rims of her glasses wielded plastic laser beams with tiny cameras mounted on the points. You could hear a zapping crackle each time she raised her bid. She was wearing a navy leather jacket, matching navy heels, and was smoking a cigarette. Needless to say, she garnered curious stares from the plainer people of the valley. Perhaps we were all feeling protective of the house's new owner and jealous of the leather lady's bidding powers, when the auction suddenly and suspiciously halted. Where were her hands? Were her eyes blinking in secret codes? What was she hiding? Like drenched sweaters hanging on a coat rack, we wanted to drop but could not. We dangled instead inside the gulp of a hiccup.

This being our first auction, my brother had explained that sellers had the right of refusal. The sellers could decide at the last minute not to sell, if a reserve was not met. The reserve, we learned, was the lowest amount acceptable by the owners. Apparently, the Knapp's reserve had not been met yet. The auctioneer announced that he and the owners would have to renegotiate terms of the sale. They went inside and left us outside, holding onto shallow and baited breath. There was a foreboding chance that the auction would be canceled. We could not make sense of things. We didn't have enough oxygen to even filter through a thought. We simply waited, dug into the wet ground with our soles, and whittled away at a piece of bark with our chattering teeth. Twenty agonizing minutes passed before hearing back from the auctioneer. He tested his mic for feedback and then tested his throat for phlegm. He looked casually over at us and said, "Folks, we'll have to start the bidding all over again."

"Seriously?" I yelped.

The nonverbal flailing resumed, right where it left off. It felt like we were in extra innings at the World Series: Dawn is at the plate with a full count, two down, and runner on third. And I'm screaming on the inside, squeezing my hands and freezing my eyes. When the auctioneer finally restarted the bidding, it was now at one thousand dollar increments. He was trying to up the ante any way he could. Meanwhile, Dawn's parents were busily pacing in small steps beside the huge tree. Even though they were nervous, they stood behind us just in case either of us needed to land safely on their shoulders. Fortunately, Dawn held the last and high-est bid, and the most fossilized, exasperated countenance.

The auctioneer wiped his brow with his red-checkered flannel sleeve and swept his arm under the rim of his baseball cap. "Come on, folks; this here is a mighty fine house. They don't come 'round here like this that often." He expressed some frustration and im-plored us to dig deep into our piggy banks. "This house, after all, is no ordinary house." He went on to detail the finer features of the home, including the stone bridge, stone patio, the acreage, wooden floors, the Kohler fixtures, brass lamps, and so forth. "Offer another thousand if that's what it takes," I instructed Dawn as we neared our own limit. "We're already the highest bidder," she murmured, making sure no one else could eavesdrop. But I couldn't believe her. I was having a hard time entrusting my future to the gesture of a hand. Yelling the bids in full throttle would have felt more natural and secure to me. Spoken words are more accurately interpretable than winks and nods and gestures. Still, nobody was speaking. Yet nobody was speechless.

On the other side of the big oak, I noticed an Amish man peeking at me. At first, I could have sworn he was my grandfather wearing a beard. Or it might have been my great uncle Mike, Zio Michello, my grandfather's twin brother. He had the smile of Santa Claus, the nose of a fairy, and the eyes of an angel. As he caught my attention with his shimmer, my heart took a snap shot. It had been a long time since I had seen my grandfather this close. I was fourteen when he died. He was as perfect then as he appeared now. Whoever he was, right then and there, I wanted to take him home with me—wherever that might be! Nonetheless, his visage calmed me. Time alone on that stone bridge earlier might have grounded or elevated the mirage because, when I looked again for the bearded man, he was gone.

With a sudden and eerie hush, the bidding stopped again. At once we, along with the curious crowd, turned our heads to the auctioneer to question the suspicious silence. No more finger waves. No more head nods. No more sighs. Not a whimper. Despite all of this frantic frenzy, had we finally arrived? The fast-speaking man slowed his

GRACE M. FALA, PHD

tongue. He tapped the microphone and sharpened his voice for that familiar yet hesitant seduction, "Going once! Going twice! Sold to the highest bidder!" He kissed that baby goodbye. With a piercing focus, the auctioneer pointed directly at Dawn and knighted her with his gavel.

Dawn and I fell fast into each other's arms and wept. Even the relief was unbearable. While in a haze, we exchanged hugs with her parents, who also shared a budding giddiness with us. None of us could gaze too long at the other without breaking up. After all, we had just barely survived a close encounter together.

A small group of onlookers circled around us. Patty Knapp congratulated us immediately and quipped, "If this is your response to winning, what would have happened if you lost?" A good question! George and Patty surrendered the fort with a hug and tearful smile. Immediately following that sweet "sold" sound, the assembly of outsiders transitioned into a gathering of new neighbors—those who lived nearby, inquisitive to meet the newcomers who would soon be moving next door.

Amish and Mennonite mostly, their aim was oddly traditional yet refreshingly humane. In single file, they lined up and down the driveway and one by one introduced themselves and welcomed us to their neighborhood. (Although with expansive acreage of farms, I wasn't quite sure how a "neighborhood," if any, existed.) They stood dutifully, like in a recess line at a busy schoolyard. Dawn and I felt thankful and humbled that they had waited in the drizzle to greet us. Their welcoming was one of the more poignant moments of the night. We also noticed that, perhaps because we were women, the women initiated introductions of themselves, their husbands, and then their children. The men led the discussion only when wives were not available or possibly deceased. With warm smiles and hardy handshakes, they extended themselves to us. I was moved by how callused and chalky some hands had become, like my grandfather's, to the touch. The sun had weathered their faces, making their smiles all the more organic. Unexpectedly, I was staring at the childhoods of my grandparents, who tilled soil and planted crops before emigrating in their youth to the States. From them, I learned to respect elders. Not that our new neighbors are chronologically old, mind you; it's just that their cultural age goes back generations. Quite naturally then, respect got rubbed into every handshake.

Our greeters seemed to already know a lot about us; the Knapps might have told them. Apparently, the Knapps were on a spiritual journey all their own—one that fortunately included us. More than a few commented that, "You're schoolteachers, aren't you? Well, the other gals who used to live here were teachers too." One woman kindly suggested, "Isn't it something? The woman who used to live here? Her name was Grace, too." Folks seemed truly charmed that the "gals" were back. We somehow already fit.

As they sauntered down the long driveway and into the engulfing darkness toward their homes, we marveled at how many of the children were barefoot. *Finally,* I thought. *A place where I can wear my cowboy hat, get scruffy, and go shoeless!*

The first moment we were alone, I seized the opportunity to present Dawn with a special surprise. Handing her a small bouquet of flowers with a balloon attached, I flaunted, "Hey, by the way, Happy Birthday. Have a house!" Dawn, who shares all household expenses with me, allowed my flexing machismo to fan itself. She reached for her gifts with a smile afire in her eyes. Seconds later, George and Patty told us they were pleased that we were the ones to procure their home, and that "Grace and Franny would be pleased too."

We went inside the house to sign the papers. I called my brother from a borrowed cell phone that hardly got reception. By representing us as our lawyer via airwaves, Herman was the first from my family to hear. He had me read portions of the contract over the phone to make sure we were legally secure. With a watchful eye and attentive heart, he guarded us like an archangel would. Immediately after, I called my mother, of course.

We later went out to dinner in celebration of Dawn's birthday and in appreciation of this grand moment of life. Dawn's parents were jubilant with us. When it comes to bouncing, they're good to go. While at dinner, conversations became daydreams. Sentences became fragments. Words turned into windows. Water, into wine. Smiles, into fantasies. Not surprisingly, we used our hands to gesture more often that night too. Apparently, the practice did us some good! In fact, we might have used our fingers, gnawed at the bones, and misplaced basic manners at dinner. Nobody seemed to notice that we were levitating. Nobody, that is, other than Grace and Frances.

CHAPTER 11

Imagine

A few days slipped by in a dream. Hardly waking, we realized that there were fewer than thirty days left to complete the legal transactions. We lost time dazing and working and now the clock was ticking. We quickly put the house in Boalsburg up for sale and began to investigate mortgage rates for the house in Belleville. Getting an accurate appraisal of a house this unique in a rural setting proved more of a challenge than expected. There were no other homes being sold with which to compare it. Not until the eleventh hour did the appraisal finally arrive. When it did, we thought we had lost the house; the appraisal was considerably lower than what we paid. Fortunately, though, a local banker knew the home and knew of its reputation. He held the home in high esteem and granted the mortgage we needed. By day thirty, with both families beside us and on angels' wings, we would be landing at Stonebridge.

Before closing the legal deal, however, we would have to close a soulful one. We had to visit Grace at Valley View. The mythical grand lady was waiting. With each passing hour, we came closer to meeting the infamous gardener. Stories about Grace only quickened our sentiments.

Even though drives from Boalsburg to Belleville were becoming routine by now, the view remained glorious with each spin of the tire. As we entered the Valley View Retirement Community, both wheels and hearts accelerated. We didn't quite know what to expect. Like awkward teenagers, Dawn and I instigated each other to go first. Since her nudge was more persuasive, I tiptoed into the lead. Dawn followed, carrying a small gift for greetings. She brought Grace a homemade jar of jam topped with gingham fabric and a bag of cookies tied with purple ribbon, curled by the wisp of scissors. Artist would finally meet artist today, face-to-face.

We hedged our way through the wide electronic doors and into a clean, powdery lobby where matching furniture framed the pastel halls. As newcomers would, we waited quietly for the receptionist to finish a phone call before introducing ourselves. With her pointing finger, the lady directed us to Grace Straley's room and commented that, "Grace has been waiting for you." We had called ahead and scheduled an appointment that, it turns out, might have been a mistake. Grace was told to expect visitors that day, but since our names were unfamiliar, she had no clue who her phantom guests would be. Indeed, our souls had already met; might this be love at first sight too? I couldn't help but wonder who or what Grace was envisioning.

We should not have been jolted then, even though we were, that Grace was unsettled to meet us. After all, we were strangers without purpose, introducing ourselves for no apparent reason. Dawn grew quiet. I tried using my voice and body tone to calm the moment. This might have been one of Grace's unclear days—or one of mine. By calling ahead, Grace might have had to endure an unnecessarily lengthy anticipation of visitors she did not recognize.

I tried to explain who we were and that we would soon be living at her old house—that, like her and Frances, Dawn and I were both schoolteachers. Like her and Frances, one of us was an artist and the other, a writer. She seemed to perk up only when we mentioned the house. She asked us repeatedly for our names. Like a teacher, she instructed us to write our names down on the back of a picture that was in the drawer. It happened to be a photograph of a younger Grace shoveling snow at Stonebridge.

With care, I asked twice about Frances. Both times, she responded with a courteous sadness, "That was a long time ago." In an effort to cultivate common ground and trust between us, I explained that Dawn and I shared a relationship perhaps a lot like that of her and Frances. There was a lull. She did not comment. But she studied us like fire.

She continued to look with intrigue at Dawn and repeatedly asked who she was. It appeared that she was drawn to Dawn's youth and vibrancy. Dawn remained quiet as they studied each other. Grace had a beauty of her own. She did not wear glasses or use a cane. Other than an occasional lapse of memory, she seemed to manage sufficiently on her own. Teaching, painting, gardening, and building a stone bridge had treated her well. Her eyes sparkled in Mediterranean blue and her shoulder-length hair was slated in a quarry of rich limestone. I felt strangely close. Were we family? Even though I knew we could not be related, I still looked for a resemblance. While she matched my height, weight, and complexion, she was boldly in a league of her own.

Her room was modest and sparse. Other than one oil painting, her walls were bare. Not incidentally, the painting was of Stonebridge. And it was not one of hers. I referred to the picture as a prop to illustrate our story. Then I asked her who had painted it, but she did not reply. There were only two visual images in her room. One was a photograph of the house—the other, a painting of it. Stonebridge obviously meant the world to her.

Dinnertime was rolling around at Valley View, so we motioned to leave. Eager to stroll the grounds, hear her stories, and become friends, we invited Grace back to the house for a visit sometime after settlement. Her response to this invitation was the clearest connection we made that hour. She said, "I'd have to check with my doctor. I'm not sure if it would be good for me. I'm not sure if I can handle it." Dawn and I reached for her with our eyes. We told her that we understood and that perhaps a visit another time would be best. We asked her just to think about it and assured her that we would respect her doctor's advice. Either way, we promised we'd be back to visit again soon.

We drove away heavyhearted, reviewing captions of each moment with Grace. A sad silence set in. While gazing at the lush views through the passenger-side window, my mind started to roam. I couldn't help but wonder what life had been like for the two audacious trailblazers—for two single women living together in a rural valley among the Amish? For two muses—one a poet, the other, an artist—trying to take flight? How did their families respond to their nontraditional lives?

We had heard through friends that, early on, the administration at Valley View actually considered barring Grace and Frances from living together in the same room because they weren't a married couple. Never mind that they were in their eighties. Never mind that they had lived together for well over fifty years. Never mind that they had loved together for over sixty years. Thank goodness and thank the spunky spines of two pioneering women, the administration reconsidered.

While leaving the valley that day, I returned to that full-length film in my mind featuring Grace and Fran. The image of Grace shoveling mounds of waist-deep snow left an imprint. I imagined them both plowing their way out... from the blizzards of life. All one need do is walk through the house to be convinced that they must have faced hardship with unnerving dignity.

Grace Straley in her youth

Frances Barnes in her youth

GRACE M. FALA, PHD

Grace & Fran at the Grand Canyon

Frances in the gardens

Grace in the gardens

Frances and Grace

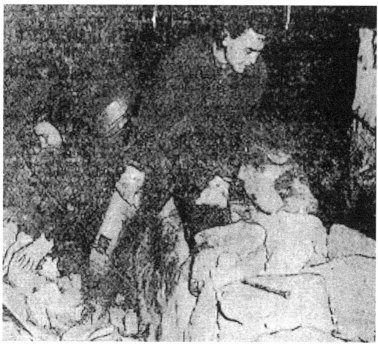

Grace and Frances building the bridge

Grace Straley

GRACE M. FALA, PHD

Frances and Grace in Hawaii

Grace at Stonebridge with Eddy, their cat

Grace in jeans, with her sisters

GRACE M. FALA, PHD

CHAPTER 12

GRACE THE DAWN

Our next visit would be on a clear day a few weeks later, a few weeks before settlement. This time, we would bring banana nut bread that Dawn baked in the shape of cupcakes. And this time, we would arrive unannounced. Upon entering, Grace happened to be in the lobby receiving a blessing from a local minister. When his hands descended onto her head, she bowed as he prayed over her. We enjoyed waiting our turn while watching beauty unfold in their exchange.

The minister left Grace with a warm afterglow. Without hesitation, we smiled as we approached her. She seemed to remember us or, if not, she seemed to trust us. Whether our communication was rooted in memory or rooted in faith, it didn't matter. We connected. Like the ebb and flow of the tides, our movement toward each other felt natural and perfectly timed. The minister, that blessing, might have helped too. We handed her the banana bread cupcakes and reminded her of our names. She wanted to know why we didn't bring cupcakes for ourselves. If we had, she would have had enough to share with us. Grace wanted to give us a gift too; she immediately wanted to give what she had just received.

Both of us were tickled to meet the clear and feisty Grace. Like old friends, she reached under our arms, latched on, and walked with us, not to lean, but with affection, to lead. Her footsteps were rhythmic and her words melodic. There was a particular place she seemed to be taking us. It would be her personal, gracious way of greeting us with a present we all could share. There might not have been enough cupcakes to go around, but Grace found something that was just as hospitable. She invited us to sit with her outside in the courtyard. True to her reputation, she called this special spot her "garden."

Grace opted to sit in the shade, though she clearly emulated the sun. We grabbed a few patio chairs and set them in an open square of warm light. A soft, green turf was hedged in by neatly manicured bushes and lined with colorful summer flora. Less like a teacher and more like a friend, the gardener tested our knowledge of the flowers. Not so much to see if we could identify their names, but more to see if we knew their spirits. In naming the flowers, I apparently impressed myself more than I impressed her. After all, it was because of Grace and Fran's notorious arboretum that my new interest in plants was even budding. She did not correct me when guessing names, though; names didn't really matter. She fancied more the way I regarded the flowers—the way I felt about them.

While I could not wow Grace with my pretentious knowledge of the gaudy sprouts, I caught her attention with some flirtation. Like a tightrope trickster, I balanced myself along a single row of bricks that lined the walkway. She followed me with her eyes laughing. She somehow knew that I would learn about flowers more with body than mind anyway. After all, names don't give flowers value. Fragrance does. And how they play tricksters themselves. An impish Grace enjoyed the playfulness.

Dawn was also more talkative this visit. While bridging together their passions for art, Grace smiled with curiosity and stared searchingly at Dawn. "Which one is the artist?" she asked again, with some confusion. "I am." Dawn replied. "What do you draw?" Grace continued. Dawn talked about her fondness for water colors and other art mediums. Grace then wanted to know what Dawn taught, where she taught, and if she enjoyed teaching. Dawn delighted in sharing pedagogical insights with her.

Three hours in the garden gave us ample time to revisit our story of Stonebridge. Seeing Grace blessed earlier by the cleric, I chose to describe the house phenomenon as a miracle. "That house, your house,

Grace, called us to it," I explained. "That house, your house, found us. We might not have the keys yet, but we have acquired its legacy. We are humbled by its story, especially as it includes you, Grace." She listened and received us with the reverence she had given the minister that morning. She could hopefully sense from our words how we had surrendered ourselves to this miracle. After a long, tender pause, we expressed our gratitude to her and Fran for the bounty of flowers and ground coverings, for the artwork, stonework, and especially for their prayers that drew us there—the ones that, out of the blue, were becoming mysteriously realized in us. And just as wondrously, our prayers were being expressed through them. Angels must have drawn us all together. When blessings are this bizarre, angels are simply making sure that you get their message. Either that, or they must have good reason for considering us thickheaded! Once the awe awakened as it did, it settled in stone.

Later, we reached for Grace on another level. We described our relationship again to be similar to that which she might have shared with Frances. The senior artist responded with receptive and loving eyes only and without words. Any mention of Frances still touched tenderness too close and too far for words. One thing she did say though, more than once, was that "we built the bridge, you know. We built the bridge." Frances finally entered the conversation with Grace's proud use of the pronoun "we." For such a resourceful term, when "we" is used by two women and even more so, two men, reactions can be cruel. Not everybody gets to use the word "we" equally. For individuals who identify as queer, for example, "we" often gets silenced and reduced to "I" in conversations and hence realities. The upkeep to protect or to liberate oneself by choosing words creatively can give independent thinkers like Grace and Frances a honed skill for communication.

Noticing this, Dawn's response affirmed Grace's disclosure of "we" and inclusion of Fran. "It's not only amazing work, Grace. The bridge is beautiful too, like the two gals who built it." She then winked and waited. Their smiles arced into a full rainbow before melting into the earth like dew. Grace and Dawn validated their names as conversation danced between them. In this poetic presence of Eros, we trusted the moment to last forever.

An announcement over the loudspeaker prompted us to make our way back. We asked Grace if she had thought about our invitation to return to Stonebridge. We really wanted her to visit if her doctor agreed. With alert eyes, she quipped, "Who cares what the doctor says. Let's go right now. I'm ready!" A complete turnaround from the previous visit, she headed toward the exit. I had to catch up. "Grace," I giggled, reminding her, "We don't have the keys yet. It's not official until the end of June. Once we're moved in, though, we're coming to get you. We want to spend an entire day with you. We'll have tea sandwiches, sit outside, and talk."

"Why can't we go today?" she asked again. Our hearts commingled with a longing for Stonebridge.

Goodbye sentiments stretched into a thick, gooey mess. After prying away, I walked halfway down the hallway before running back. I felt desperate to hug her once more. She obliged. I held her for a loving moment and whispered close to her ear, "Thank you. Thank you so much, Grace. I'm so proud to have met you." With an inquisitive pause, "What did I do that you should be proud?" she quipped, making sure not to end an interrogative statement with a preposition. I looked at her piercing blue eyes and welled up. Then I kissed her hands, smiled slowly, and ran down the hall to where Dawn was tearfully waiting. "If only you knew, Grace," I sighed while peeking back one last time at her.

While sprinting out, I almost bumped into a butterfly passing through the automatic door, going Grace's direction. She would surely see it. She was not one to ever miss any of nature's magic.

CHAPTER 13

YOU ALREADY HAVE WHAT YOU NEED

August Day

The chipmunk small
Has aestivated.
The cow's cud
Is masticated.
A rainy day
Is adumbrated,
But this big rock
Is elevated.

The horse cropped grass
And meditated.
I sat on the rock
And vegetated,
But the energy was generated:

I picked one berry,
But Esther ate it.

Grace enjoyed bantering about her birthday. She was born on August 8, 1908. Toying with the number eight as a mnemonic device, she etched the auspicious date into memory. Her birthday was soon approaching. While packing, we found a new, handmade coffee mug with the name "Grace" printed in calligraphy on it. After filling it with chocolates and sweets, we set it aside for a surprise visit on her birthday. We also made sure there were plenty of goodies for Grace to share back with us. Our dreams of being closer to her remained as we packed and boxed, sorted and lifted, and slept soundly each night.

On June 28, one week after closing, we finally moved in. With access to a large U-Haul and a couple of strong college students, we loaded in Boalsburg and unloaded in Belleville. If we didn't get the truck back to the rental company by seven o'clock, we'd be charged another day's rental. It was already six by the time we finished unloading. After a hurried, hot, and sticky day, Dawn and I were depleted. If we could push for just one more hour, we could make it back in time. But that infamous second wind was not blowing. Something held us back and effectively stopped us in our tracks.

The sun started to set in sweet holiness. We had hurried feverishly all day to return that truck in time, but it had become physically and soulfully impossible to leave the magnetic views of the sunset. Dawn and I decided to absorb the extra expense for the truck just so we could sit and gaze into the wonder. We were held and rocked by the peacefulness that followed and treated to eyelash kisses from the breeze.

With ears cupping the wind, we could hear the melodic clip-clop of passing hooves. The sound was lovely. We sighed "hallelujah" for the much-needed moment of calm. Then, realizing that this might be a new neighbor, a potential friend, we waved like kids flagging down the popsicle man until the buggy passed. Amazement shook us. How is it that we are living here? Were we actually called to this blessed place? Could we ever be thankful enough? Will that view ever be believable? We were now here. Here is where the sun plays and the wheat waves. The corn claps and the hills roll. Here is where the view visits the viewer with a caress that lingers through the body before reentering earth. Here is where we plant love and take root.

The next morning when we drove the U-Haul back to the garage, we felt slightly apologetic to be returning it late. It might have been that same aura of enduring hues that prompted the manager to wink and offer, "No extra charge, ladies. This one's on me." Could it be? How did he know? Had he been kissed by that sunset too? Apparently, staying with color and light was precisely what we were meant to do! After conveying our gratitude with tempered exuberance, we headed back to Big Valley. Strange how, at times, it seemed as though we were wearing a fragrance that instantly attracts kindness from others, anyone really, like Obi Wan Kenobi's telepathic allure in *Star Wars*.

The Fourth of July weekend was soon upon us. My mother, sisters, and two preteen nephews drove to Belleville to help us unpack during what was reported to be the hottest week of the century—and it's 1999! Fortunately, we were good humored about the intense heat. Not much of a choice, I suppose. In sweltering heat, nothing incidental matters. The air is simply too heavy and thick to fuss over anything other than basic essentials. We worked like bodies without thoughts. Lift. Load. Unload. Trash. Without any breeze and hardly enough breath, we didn't talk or laugh much either. Despite the sweat-festering sacrifice, family troopers remained stalwart. After all, it was Sunday, the Fourth of July. They could have been home watching fireworks in the cool shade or watching television in air-conditioned rooms. Our new abode, while shaded under a canopy of majestic oaks, has no refrigerant to cool it and no TV for escape. The heat weighed so heavily, even gratitude got sappy.

Later that night my young nephews, Ryan and Andrew, and I planned to celebrate the occasion in a more traditional style. Earlier that weekend, we had stopped by a makeshift roadside stand to purchase select fireworks. Pennsylvania has strict laws regarding the potency of such explosives. I assumed that our selection of sparklers and smoke snakes fell within the parameters of the law. Faulty assumptions never cease to amaze me, however.

For the best possible light show, we waited until darkness settled. In a conscientious and tactful manner, Ryan reminded his aunt of necessary safety precautions. He accurately figured his aunt would be carefree and wily. After all, one of us—at least—should assume the role of adult. So before striking the first match, and with Ryan's advice, we filled a large bucket of water, unraveled the hose, and dragged it through the tall grass to a barren stone foundation. This framed desolate area was where George and Patty were going to build their horse barn and likely where Dawn and I build ours.

Andrew, the younger of the two, studied the wind for direction. Then he caught a fast glimpse of a bat's ballet. Bats were flirting with the night and swooping into open spaces like Mighty Mouse. Andrew kept pace and watched in fascination. He was visibly wowed by their fierce elegance. The bat dance made it easier to ignite our imaginations too. One by one, I lit the wick of each bottle rocket before all three of us jumped back as if we were releasing a lion into the wilderness. After the first explosion, it was clear that these were no ordinary Pennsylvania dazzlers. They must have been smuggled in for unlawful sales. We thought twice only briefly before leaping unabashedly into the thrills again.

Even as we cracked a thunderous noise and set the sky aglow that Sunday night, we couldn't help but wonder why the rest of the valley was so quiet. Where were all the other revelers, all the other boomers? We scanned the sky repeatedly, but not a spark. There wasn't even a distant display. We strutted proud to have provided the valley with the noise and glimmer of American independence. The neighbors might even thank and applaud us tomorrow.

Besides our own, the only fireworks visible that night were illuminated by Andrew's poetic ten-year-old spirit. Later that evening, he and I sat on rocking chairs in front of the house and reviewed the dangerous skirmishes of an hour ago. We calmly entertained the darkness with openhearted conversation. The stars were winking and fireflies blinking. My heart stretched as Andrew reached for the magic in the moment. "Aunt Grace, do you see those trees down there? See them? Aren't they cool! Who needs fireworks? We have all the fireworks anyone could ever need. All you have to do is just watch the fireflies in the trees. They're like constellations of stars descending onto the branches." His loving creativity was convincing. "Yes, Andrew," I agreed. "It is really, really cool." (At least we found something cool!) We sat and watched the constellation of stars twinkling from the old oak trees. After all, it was the Fourth of July.

The next day shed even more light on the night before. While driving to the local hardware shop, we spotted a few inconspicuous tree signs. "No Sunday fishing." "Closed Sundays." "No Sunday Sales." Could it be? Don't tell me. In no time, we discovered a lifestyle that reflects long-standing religious customs and cultural traditions: Sunday is still considered a day of rest in the valley. I had heard that people from the old country in the old days used to honor Sundays with veneration. It had never occurred to me that this valley is indeed that old country, from those old days. How could I ever face the neighbors now? We had naively and loudly introduced our Sunday selves to the neighborhood the night before. We entered with a bang.

CHAPTER 14

BE A PRAYER

Dandelion Ghosts

I came down the hill
As the dusk drifted down,
Misty and cool and gray.
The round, pale ghosts
Of the dandelion heads
Leaned toward me and seemed to say
In a sibilant whisper, all secret and soft,
"Here's the one stole our sisters away."
Then their hair floated toward me
And caught at my gown
As a rustling breeze wafted
Their gossamer down
In swirls round my face.
I stiffened and listened,
My feet tensed to race,
As the ghosts whispered,
"Who-o-o-o,
Who-o-o-o,
Who-o-o-o,
Who-o-o-o,
Who stole our sisters away?"

Summer days passed in a haze. Though most boxes were emptied by now, Dawn and I were still settling. We were amazed at how mix-and-match furnishings that were out of place at our former house happened to fit perfectly at Stonebridge. Like parenting the prodigal dressers, our furniture had waited years before coming home to their rightful rooms. Relief and celebration welcomed the homecoming of bed, chair, and bookshelf. Just as I had envisioned during that long, reflective drive to Shippensburg weeks prior, except for a few items—a lamp, a ladder, and a few wall hangings, our new abode was fully furnished. We were finally ready to pick up Grace and, simply, to bring her home on a sunny day.

Beforehand though, we called Ken, the father of a new neighbor, to help with our unexpected midsummer plumbing problems. Due to the intense heat and foreboding drought, the well water had become dull and murky. Dawn and I had learned that whenever a neighbor or a relative thereof can serve you, there's an unspoken expectation to go through the valley channels especially since, if not acquaintances, folks are likely related somehow. Neighbors with surnames of Peachey, Yoder, Hostetler, Swarey, and Zook have lived in the valley for generations. So it would be best (and proper) to talk with a local expert, of course! Once Ken finished the diagnostics, we would leave for Valley View to be with Grace and to be held by her stories of Stonebridge. What might she have to teach us about well water woes? These pipes? Those trails? The old gardens? The neighborhood? Even if in an Alzheimer's fog, we eagerly sought her attention and affections. Anticipation tickled our toes. Our dreams of being with Grace had ripened and were ready for picking. It was important to us that she feel rooted at home again.

Our excitement grew as Ken neared completion of his work. With impetuosity, we grabbed the "Grace" mug filled with candies to show Ken. "Look! Look what we're bringing to Grace Straley today. She's one of the ladies who used to live here. Do you know her?" While retrieving a plumber's fishing line from the well, Ken spoke softly, "Grace, oh sure, I knew her. You'd always see her working in that garden back there." He used his head and shrugged our attention toward the backyard. "I remember her hiking through those woods, day in and day out, working out back. Did you know she used to wear men's work boots? I'll tell you, those two gals really knew their flowers though." He paused momentarily and looked up to say, "They were good people, Grace and Fran. It seems only fitting that the two of you should be here now. Did you know that they were schoolteachers too?" Since everyone's kin, it seemed everyone already knew the headlines of our lives. Plus, being like Grace and Fran was all most folks needed to know, or all anyone really wanted to know.

He didn't pause to continue though I had hoped he had. "I'm pretty sure Grace passed on a few weeks back."

"No, you have them confused," I quickly corrected him, certain that he was mistaken. "That was Frances. Frances passed on a few years ago, but Grace still lives. In fact, we've been to visit her a few times, and we're going back to Valley View today for another visit."

"No, no." Ken persisted. "I'm pretty sure it was Grace who passed."

Refusing to hear, I then insisted. "It's Frances who has died, Ken. Grace still lives."

He stopped his plumbing and looked with intention into our eyes. "I'm sure it was Grace. You see, you might not know this, but my wife works at Valley View. She helps out at the reception desk."

Dawn and I gasped, riveted to the ground. Neither of us could move, let alone speak. My heart began trembling with dry palpitations, skipping through breath like pebbles over a wasteland. With my body in a quiver and mind floating away, I could not believe him. After all, who is this guy we just met? Grace is still waiting for us. I'm sure of it. She knows of our plans to bring her home. Still and chilled, we sat in silence and waited for Ken to finish. We could not speak. It was impossible to say anything more than "thank you" to him as he was leaving.

As soon as he pulled away, Dawn and I looked frightfully at each other and found our way back inside the house. "Call," I implored. "Can you call? Can you call Valley View to find out for sure?" I knew I couldn't do it. Dawn nodded in fixed silence. She composed herself while flipping through the phone book to find the number. I caught a prayer with my hands and clenched it until it vanished. With a shuddering softness, Dawn spoke to the attendant. Her body language indicated that it was true. "Ask when!" I urged. "Find out exactly where and when." I was desperate to know, while at the same time, something inexplicably beautiful gave me pause, like the grace of a baby's smile. But it was strange too.

"She did die," Dawn confirmed, biting her lip as she hung up the phone.

A tearful silence broke. "How? When? Where? What did the lady say?" I interrogated.

Dawn's response was slow, delicate, and measured. "June 28. Late afternoon, early evening, sometime between six and seven... Outside... in the garden... in the courtyard... where we were with her." She paused and blanked before continuing. "The lady said that she died peacefully." Words fell hollow. Sounds, barren. Breath, shallow. We sat and cried arid tears until our great loss hit us. Then the wet tears flowed. The poignancy of the moment revealed itself with a tremor.

June 28 was the day we moved in and the same day we felt compelled to heed the blessings of that beautiful setting sun. We yielded our worries to the majestic view that visited us that day. We weren't even charged the next day for the U-Haul. Perhaps that same setting sun actually had visited that shop manager after all? And Grace? Where and when did she die? Could it be? A knowing suddenly hovered over us and comforted us like a shroud: the same day we moved into Stonebridge, Grace exited life.

Grace passed the torch to us the hour she died. She ran her last emotional marathon. Mounting one last stone on her bridge, clearing one more twig from her walking trail, she breathed deeply the fragrance of her favorite wild flowers and hiked the mountainside one more time. And then, bowing gracefully to us and possibly, for us, through the rich hues of a setting sun, she departed just as an artist of nature would.

Now whenever I see the perceptual trickery of a setting sun, I wonder if the sky is actually drawing its curtains—if all those who have died that day have orchestrated their timely and graceful surrender like Grace did. Just before they go to rest peacefully, I imagine them taking bows or giving curtsies. Some whisk their names with whimsical strokes in every inconceivable language. Others swirl designs in calligraphy. Others, yet still, sweep their creative X on the spot. Their names remain etched in the sky. Their bows remain nudges in the wind. Grace abides there now. There but for the Grace of you go I. We who are honored to witness such grandeur lower our heads and awaken our hearts with a whisper, "Bravo, dear brothers. Brava, my sisters. Encore, loving friends. Thank you."

Dawn and I allowed the sadness to hold us and trusted the silence to feed us. We went about the day in a different tempo, with our insides out. Yesterday we bounced; today, we glide. Yesterday we planned; today, we surrender. Yesterday, we chatted; today, we chant. It was—we were—softer and quieter. A rhythm was already present; all we did was step into the dance. And reside in a prayer.

Simple truths awaken in the air we breathe. I could sense something presenting itself, like a flower in springtime. I asked Dawn, "What about the memorial service for Grace? Did we miss it? We were in the middle of moving. We probably missed the service." Such a deduction would have been logical, I know, especially since she died a few weeks ago by now. But I no sooner asked the question, when I knew the answer. I knew something, yet did not know how I knew. From an academic perspective, I was ruminating—not knowing. Valid deductions before drawing them, and not much less, before speaking them must be supported. I clearly had no support for my bold, sweeping claim. But I knew something clearly nonetheless, which for me is in itself unusual. I knew Grace's last wish. It was planted in my heart, sprouting in my mind and on my lips.

Still I hesitated and needed confirmation. Twirling my hair while pacing, I asked Dawn to call back right away to inquire about the memorial services. She kindly obliged and didn't even ask why. My body language suggested that I was on to something. Dawn soon discovered that Valley View had not held the memorial service yet. Grace died on June 28. It was mid-July by now. What was the delay? The time differential would have come as a surprise to most people, but not to me. Dawn explained that the family had requested that Grace be commemorated on August 6. This allowed family members from out-of-state sufficient time to return from traveling and vacationing. To our astonishment, this also gave us opportunity to learn of Grace's death and to attend her funeral service. My heart was clear and the timing perfect. I wanted her home, back at Stonebridge.

Fran and Grace lived lives as risk-takers. Grace possibly wanted one last chance to kick-start a generation into recognizing themselves more honestly. She might have forged through social and religious taboos one last time by deciding to be cremated. Cremations are rather unusual in the valley. Her proud defiance blazed a trail once again. Dawn and I wondered how her relatives were handling the blaze. Neither of us had ever met Grace's relatives. Her memorial arrangements were out of our hands but not out of reach. I wished her home and somehow knew she would accept. In an instant that presented itself as an eternity, Grace and I wished the same wish, prayed the same prayer, spoke to God with the same voice, and shared the same breath. I told Dawn and, of course, I told my mother, "We have to spread her ashes here. This is where she belongs. I'm sure of it." I knew that what I was saying could be perceived as bizarre. But the clarity in my heart was unwavering. Both Dawn and Rose appreciate how mystery and humility walk hand in hand. For a message this sensitive, it is wise to choose an understanding receiver. Once again, I heeded my mother's kindhearted advice. She reminded me to "let it go. See what happens. If it's meant to be, it will be." I did just that and said nothing more about it. All that was left was trust as we wait for August 6.

CHAPTER 15

Play with Paradox

A house sold at auction is usually sold "as is," with no guarantees. This did not concern us that much. The Knapps had left the interior of the house in beautiful condition. Fresh paint framed the new fixtures. The hardwood flooring was sanded and polished; plus, linoleum was installed on kitchen and bath floors. Dawn and I planned to someday paint the exterior of the home and to renovate the two attics. Before doing anything major, however, we had to clear the garage. It was piled up so high and deep that navigating it would be akin to climbing Mount Everest. Grace and Fran, and subsequently George and Patty, left behind old tools, lumber, paint cans, dispensers, and loose paraphernalia. Teachers tend to collect a lot of supplies too—books, props, handouts, articles—so Dawn and I dug our feet into the debris and began to burrow some additional space.

As excavations of Stonebridge continued, there were still adjustments outsiders like us had to make. The rhythms and routines of rural life were completely different from any we had ever known. Hardly a month had passed since we had moved. I was already longing for crusty French or Italian bread, homemade pasta, sharp provolone, the local delivery of pizza—or local delivery of anything, for that matter. Access to the *New York Times* or the *Washington Post* or any kind of ethnic cuisine would also be nice. None would be available perhaps forevermore in Big Valley, for all I knew. What a relief to discover that we were on route for trash collection! We might be the only ones in the area that would even consider trash pickup. Like generations before them, many neighbors still reuse, compost, or burn. Luckily, we are equipped with electricity, though there's no cable for television, cell service, or satellite for computer.

Like kids on a treasure hunt, we explored the garage with a spirit of discovery. There must have been five rakes made of bamboo and three made of green plastic. We fancied the rusty old wheelbarrow and looked forward to cranking the canary-yellow electric snow blower leftover from the sixties. As we emptied the treasure chest, we filled the driveway, so much so that there wasn't much room for a maroon van to drive in, curve around the new frontier of junk, and park. We didn't know who was about to enter our abandoned expedition. Whoever it was would be subjected to our sudden awareness that our disheveled, scoundrel appearance might spook them away! Hearts aflutter once again with blood pressure rising, it was an unexpected visit from our new neighbors and their five cherubs. They live on the farm across the street and to the right of us. Indeed, they probably heard the Sunday night boomers. Now they'd have a chance to see the sweat-stained looks on the faces behind the fireworks, with sleeves to match!

It took only a second to notice how our intruders wore the sun on their faces. They were dressed simply in conservative Mennonite clothing. Being with nature grants them privileges to everything natural. Their eyes glistened and cheeks radiated when they talked. Each of the five children seemed to embody similar qualities. Despite the initial panic, Dawn and I felt at ease in no time. They reintroduced themselves as Chet and Julia, reminding us that we had met the night of the auction. I remembered their rosy complexions and their glow. I could not, however, remember their names. Valley folks seem startled, if not offended, when you don't remember their names. Theirs is still very much an oral culture. Memories lock onto spoken words in ways quite different from what I observe in modern students, who are accustomed to visual, technological cues for mnemonics. One thing was both odd and clear: the locals remember your name, your church, and your words. What you say sticks.

We talked for a while and watched the sun set together. While they had developed a friendship with the Knapps and were sorry to see them leave, they were hospitable in welcoming us to the valley. Dawn and I wanted to reciprocate somehow, so we shared our personal hoard of candy stashed away for long cleaning days like these with the five bambini.

Before leaving, Chet and Julia invited us to a neighborhood gathering on Friday night. Chet explained that the neighborhood stretched from stop sign to stop sign. I'm glad he specified. Neither Dawn nor I could easily identify land boundaries among fields of farms. We didn't even know that a neighborhood could exist among such vast open spaces. Everything was whirling with change.

Chet said that the gathering would begin promptly at seven and asked us to bring one hot dish, one dessert, and a chair to sit on. He repeated the time twice before boarding his van to leave, seemingly distrustful that we would not be prompt or that we would not remember.

I wondered if valley people adhered to time differently and if Chet thought that city slickers like us might not honor arrival times. When from the suburbs, you're neither from the city nor the country. Suburbs have that dubious distinction of being some place in between or no place at all. Around the valley, we're city folks. When in the city, we're farm gals. We're neither, actually, although we enjoy learning and living the weird and wonderful, goofy and meaningful differences.

Dawn and I accepted Chet and Julia's invitation and thanked them for visiting. As soon as their van left the driveway, apprehension blew in. I looked to Dawn and freaked, "What will we bring? What do we wear? How do you dress for an Amish and Mennonite neighborhood gathering? We'll have to make something that people will actually eat. We'll be making first impressions, you know, the ones that last longest?" I had a hunch that homemade biscotti or pasta fagioli would not go over. Thank goodness that it was Monday night. We had a few days to wrestle with details.

Dawn immediately called her mother and grandmother for their expertise. They had had some prior experience with Amish culture. They advised Dawn to make homemade black-raspberry pudding and cranberry chicken with rice. "What? You're kidding, right?" I was too nervous to be easily convinced, not to mention that I had never heard of black-raspberry pudding or cranberry chicken.

So as soon as the line was free, I called my mother, a bona fide city dweller, who was born and reared in Philadelphia. Even though her parents were farmers before emigrating from Italy, Rose mostly has urban beginnings. My grandparents, both bilingual and bicultural, moved from rural to urban homes and spoke mostly Italian with broken English. During the summers of her youth, however, my mother and her family rented homes in the heart of Pennsylvania farmland where her father worked as a mining contractor. She often recalls how much she enjoyed gathering eggs from the hens and milk from the cows. While Rose has fond memories of rural life, her children, on the other hand, have solid suburban roots. No hens. No cows. No neighborhood gatherings.

When asked for advice, my mother relayed what she knew. I could hear her chewing on a cracker at the other end of the line as she replied. "Make some homemade spaghetti and meatballs. That always goes over big. That can be the main dish. And bake some cagiunes, you know, the filled cookies. They like things filled out there, don't they? I just made a batch the other day that was out of this world. Quick, grab a pen. I'll give you the recipe over the phone." I couldn't believe what I was hearing. Clearly, she had no clue. Suddenly, nobody knew me anymore. I used to be a suburban mannequin with family ties. Now I'm a rural bumpkin with a family of mannequins. They didn't quite get it. How does a misplaced Italian suburbanite outsider, who does not cook regularly and who refuses to follow a recipe, cook for a group of Amish and Mennonite farmers who have lived in this neighborhood all their lives?

Frazzled, I tried to explain to my mother that the word "spaghetti" was foreign around here and that "noodles" were more common. "So call it noodles with tomato sauce. Call it whatever you'd like. Better yet, call it what it is. It'll be good for your neighbors to get a taste of who you are too, doll baby. You can't change where you come from," she replied wisely. "Come on, Ma," I whined. "Chances are good that these folks will be our neighbors for quite a while. Not many people leave their valley roots around here. Most families have been around for generations, which is something you don't see often where you live."

Okay, maybe the spaghetti and cagiunes would go over, I thought to myself momentarily, *but they'd have to be my mother's. I have never made either dish before, and this was not the time to start.*

"Check to see what Dawn comes up with. She'll know what you can bring," my mother rightly suggested. Dawn had more confidence in her ability to create something special anyway, so I entrusted her with my lofty, perplexed expectations. Then I bit my nails.

The next day, in an effort to make more headway into the neighborhood, we brought a clock to a local Amish man for repairs. This would be the first time either of us had entered an Amish home. John and his wife, Lydia, both in their retiring years, graciously received the out-of-towners yet looked musingly at the two of us. *How many years before we're no longer outsiders?* I wondered. *Or are we talking generations?*

Simplicity charmed their home. We entered through the kitchen, where a large kerosene lamp hung from the ceiling in the middle of the room. There were no appliances, which was to be expected. But, to our surprise, there were also no pictures, no paintings, no tchotchkes, and no frills. While the furniture was old, worn, and useful, the floor and walls sparkled oddly with newness.

In preparation for lunch, more commonly referred to as dinner, Lydia stoked the stove with small bricks of ash wood. John explained how ash wood burned with an intense and enduring heat in comparison to other woods. With our first winter in the valley soon upon us, and with wood as our primary heat source, we listened intently.

We were delighted to make their acquaintance and pleased to see how simplicity teaches. Dawn and I were becoming more engaged with Amish culture, traditions, and peoples. We were observing them to be people of difference who also make a difference too.

To ease the awkward tensions between us, we introduced ourselves to John and Lydia as schoolteachers. Dawn and I had learned earlier that our occupation still holds esteem in this Amish valley. Like that of an old European village, the schoolteacher is highly regarded as instrumental in shaping the future of children. In fact, most people refer to us more as schoolteachers than as Grace and Dawn. Frankly, we enjoyed the respect our neighbors gave. (Sometimes, privately, we even think we deserve it!)

As we were leaving, Lydia asked if I would write my name and phone number on a small notepad. This also struck me curious, since most Amish customs forbid phone service in the home. Before I could think twice though, Lydia was quick to explain that she would go to a neighbor's to call when the clock was ready. So I did what she asked and handed the notepad back to Lydia. She studied my name for a moment. Then, with the ball of her finger, she smoothed over it as though reading in Braille. She then tried to pronounce, "*Faaaaaaa*-la. Fa-*laaaaaaa*. Grace Fala." She looked up and gazed inquisitively into my eyes. "You must be from overseas," she reasoned. My name must have felt foreign to her. "Well, yes," I stammered, like I had been caught. "Sort of. My grandparents were immigrants. But I was born right here in Pennsylvania." I was startled by the weirdness of the moment. Apparently I was just as foreign to her as she was to me. I recognized her earnest attempt, however, to locate me somewhere in the world she knew. Still flustered, I smiled with her and realized how new we were to each other. Frankly, I was mapping her in my world too.

As we walked out the door, Lydia leaned over, lowered her voice, held her hand over her mouth, and like a spy, looked both ways before mumbling, "Stay out of trouble. Teachers have reputations, you know." Her wit and flare tickled us into a relaxed laughter.

We enjoyed talking with John and Lydia and perhaps, because of our differences, have maintained a friendship since. We value being with them, in humor, wisdom, and poetry. Once John described a visit to the doctor's office and said the x-ray of his vertebrae looked like a "stump in fog." Another time he expressed some frustration with "Too soon, old. Too late, smart."

Usually, when I say my last name, folks hear "Fowler" and assume my affiliation as "one with the birds." There are very few, if any, names that end with a vowel in the valley. It was clear to me that if my name was different, then I was different too. If it weren't true, I'd probably find it unsettling. But it is true; I am different. Hopefully one day we can share enough commonality to be freely different.

Dawn's last name, on the other hand, resonated with greater ease for Lydia and John. She lucked out. Her name is one of the more familiar names in the area. While not as common as Yoder, Peachey, Zook, Swarey, Byler, and Hostetler, the Hayes family own a local bank. When Dawn mentions her last name, folks in the valley not only recognize it, they sometimes erroneously assume that she is among the banker's branch of the family tree. In other words, they assume she has affiliations with money. Perhaps self-fulfilling prophecies work both ways!

CHAPTER 16

FAVOR THE ONES YOU LOVE

Dandelion Gold

When last I saw this hillside
It was glowing with flowers of gold.
I gathered great bunches
And ran home to share
All the glory my hands would hold.

They blazed from the bowl on our table,
Little suns from the cool earth of May;
And their innocent brightness was able
To keep us all pleasant that day
When the dandelion gold made us gay.

Friday night was soon upon us. We decided to wear blue jean dresses to the neighborhood gathering. Dawn wore mine and I wore hers. Our dresses were unique yet plain enough not to draw too much attention. They were also casual and, hopefully, appropriate. Frankly, the dress was already a stretch for me, but at least I didn't have to wear a bonnet. Dawn did wear her hair up, though. She knows how to adapt comfortably to most situations. I tend to encourage situations to adapt to me. Tonight, however, was different. I wasn't as comfortable as she was, but I wasn't awkward either. I was resolved to let whatever happens happen.

The night was beautiful enough to experience with our toes. We decided to follow a local custom and to walk barefoot, carrying our entrées—cranberry chicken and black-raspberry pudding—romantically in picnic baskets around one arm. This way, the other arm could maneuver the folding chairs. If I were more daring, I would have swung both chairs with one hand, just to walk arm in arm with Dawn. We could skip down the driveway like best-friend schoolgirls who share lots of secrets.

It was exactly 7:00 p.m. when we got there, just as Chet instructed. Even when we were careful not to be late, it seemed as though we were last to arrive. Perhaps city folks do have different views of time? The neighborhood of guests was gathered in front of Chet and Julia's house, between two towering spruce trees that provided much-needed shade from the sun. Politeness filled the air. Roles specific to men, women, and children were implied. While women sat on one side and men on the other, the children assembled quietly and properly with their respective families. Even as modern-day schoolteachers, we hadn't witnessed such manners from children since we ourselves were kids. They sat quietly, helped out when asked, and studied us with a courteous fascination. It seemed as though everyone present had a specific script to follow, especially the kids, and except us.

Having no clue as to how to behave at such an event, I surreptitiously followed the lead of others and sat with the women. Speaking with a slight notch above a whisper, we shared details about the dishes we prepared. (I had asked Dawn earlier to fib if necessary, falsely claiming that I made one of the two dishes. Even though she deserved full credit for cooking, I was foolishly hoping to earn a little recognition for picking the black raspberries. For some reason though, berry picking doesn't really count for much. There's no recipe involved.)

Chet monitored the barbecue and the cooler of nonalcoholic beverages from one corner of the shade, while Julia tended to the various dishes brought by guests. She placed the dishes on two folding tables propped in the shadow of the two trees. One table was overflowing with casseroles, Crock-Pots, and bread baskets. The other bowed from the bounty of desserts precariously balanced on it. Last time I had seen such a rich variety of food was at a smorgasbord in Rome. While not the more familiar prosciutto with melon, penne pasta, lasagna, or antipasta, the feast before me still aroused all the senses. Every fresh vegetable and fruit was present somewhere, whether in the salads, baked dishes, homemade breads, or puddings. Shoofly pie, whoopie pies, and moon pies accompanied the freshly picked corn and cabbage entrées. While it seemed impossible to taste each delectable selection, I planned wholeheartedly to make the effort as I began to fill my plate.

When the moment was right, Chet sought our attention as a group. The big guy with corn-silk hair, sunbaked skin, and crusted farmers' hands packed a stature strong enough for bridling a six-horse team. He easily earned our gaze as soon as he announced that "it is time to bless the meal." Traditionally, if a male deacon or minister were present, he would bless the meal. If not, the man of the house does. If there's no man in the house, as was the case with Grace and Fran, and now for Dawn and me, a man present should be asked. During the blessing, Dawn and I glanced quickly over at each other to acknowledge how awkward a public prayer was. I doubly checked my body language as I peered around. Guests were silent; heads were bowed and hands still. What was awkward to us was rather familiar to the rest of the neighborhood. Looking around, I suddenly felt a strong wave of embarrassment upon realizing that I had already begun eating some time before the blessing. I imagined everyone had noticed and, if not, they must surely see how flustered I was. Then I remembered the fireworks on a Sunday night.

I was really leaving an impression now, a lot like the cartoon character Ziggy. But then I realized that references to Ziggy and other common sayings might not be relatable. Reality appeared suddenly unreal. Expressions associated with photography, television, radio, sports, Grammy Award-winning music, computer technology, and the like might need to be edited from discourse. Routine sayings that ordinarily open a path of conversation within my cultural reality might actually distance interactants here, and some might even offend. For example, comments such as "a Kodak moment," "a photo finish," "the Cha Cha Slide," "Dumbledore's Army," "phone home," "trust the force," "the Land of Oz," and "the Phillie Phanatic" might appear preposterous or unwittingly boastful. And the basic "microwave," "text," "email," "message me," and "drive-through" might make me even more estranged and English than I want to appear. Living a life of difference and being a teacher, I had become adept at selecting words creatively to foster inclusive learning climates. But these adaptations were especially challenging and turned my understandings of the world at the time upside down. Perhaps this new neighborly welcome would make the cultural assimilation easier; one could only hope!

Folks were as odd to us as it seemed we were to them. Curiosity kept us afloat though, as local customs and proprieties steered conversation more than usual. Individual personalities appeared eclipsed by group protocols. Relational roles already assumed were unfamiliar to us and hence awkward. Even the silence that stretched the chitchat made us stir. Is it my turn to talk now? Or will I be interrupting? Are we supposed to pause, to reflect? Am I blurting more than relating? What is permissible? And what is taboo? Topics that revolved around church, recipes, nature, or the valley seemed okay but still, I wasn't sure. As novices, we listened at best and, by doing so, learned that this very event was more properly a gathering than a picnic.

Even though my parents made every effort to have their seven children say grace before meals, I was unaccustomed to doing it in public, at an outdoor Amish neighborhood gathering, at sunset, in the middle of nowhere. In an effort to redeem myself, just in case somebody actually did notice, I thought that I should perhaps compliment the chefs of the delicious foods. Saying something, anything really, might help. I tested with "this casserole is really delicious! So fresh! You made this?" to the woman on my left and was greeted by an awkward and stiff half nod. Then I tried the neighbor to my right with "wow, this pie would win a ribbon at the Grange Fair, it's so good!" Nothing. Crickets.

No doubt, I should have kept quiet. It's not easy being silent though, while feeling like the guest of honor and the stranger from Neverland at the same time. My social reality began to unhinge. I looked around.

GRACE M. FALA, PHD

The compliments weren't going over. Nobody else seemed to be giving any. Maybe compliments sound boastful and complaints disrespectful? No compliments? No complaints? My Italian blood started flowing backward! I didn't quite know what to say or do. Body gestures failed me and everything natural fell completely into a cultural pit. How can we be only a three-hour drive from Philadelphia or Pittsburgh and still be so removed? What kind of a neighborhood is this anyway?

Dawn and I were not only the new kids on the block; we were easily the oddballs. Words of wisdom from Stonebridge's former resident began to resonate. Fran was known to have said, "Everybody in the valley knows everything about you. What they don't know, they make up." Waves of timidity and bashfulness flooded us. One by one, gatherers approached and reintroduced themselves, like they did the night of the auction. We observed once again how some folks seemed surprised and slightly disappointed that we had not remembered their names. Sensing this, I attempted to memorize as many names as possible.

There were approximately eleven families represented in a gathering of about thirty people. Many guests were Mennonites. Two families were Amish. Three were Beachy Amish and completely new to us. Though modest in most ways, individuals who are Beachy Amish-Mennonite tend to be more modern; they drive cars, own phones, and use electricity, although radio and television are restricted. While beards and bonnets remain similar, those who identify as Beachy Amish attend a physical church building, while the Amish in our valley, each affiliated with a specific Ordnung, use one another's farms for Sunday worship and fellowship.

As newcomers, we noticed two questions asked most frequently: Where are you from? What church do you belong to? No matter how much we fudge the answers, no matter how often we explain that suburbanites are not city dwellers, we're still known as city gals who might travel all the way to Provincetown, Cape Cod, a twelve-hour jaunt, for fellowship and sisterhood. Neither Dawn nor I mind, however. We have come to accept the ways by which our neighbors learn to value one another. We also recall days living in the suburbs. When meeting people there, questions commonly asked were: What do you do? Where do you work? We enjoyed shifting our focus from how we function to how we relate.

One question in particular that night left such sweet residue. Dawn was on one end of a conversation and I was on another when Israel, one of our new neighbors, asked if we were sisters, which, for us, is not an uncommon inquiry. Israel lives on the property next to us, to our left. He told us that he and his wife had six daughters, many of whom sat behind us at the gathering, speaking Pennsylvania Dutch. I fumbled slightly, hearing echoes from the closet of my past, and explained to Israel that, "we aren't related but," with a chuckle, "we are close enough to be sisters." He looked again and with love in his eyes and poetry in his voice, he mused, "Oh, so this is the one you favor?" Startled, I did not quite know how to respond. I even had to make sure I heard him correctly. "Yes, you could say that. She is the one I favor" I blushed. Serenity entered and an echo was quieted. Somewhere between Chet's blessing and the melodic sounds of Pennsylvania Dutch, I lost my senses and didn't notice that Israel was attempting to understand us. He then carried on the conversation with Dawn.

To this day, Israel's inquiry has been a rhetorical treasure of mine. Just to think if not for an incidental passing comment, I would have missed his affirmation. In her song *Conversation*, songwriter Joni Mitchell sings, "Love is a story told to a friend. It's second hand." With an aromatic tease, I felt a secondhand love linger into the night. For all of these made-up, perceived differences between us, Israel had found a simple, common way of asking a complex question. He created romance out of the awkward and illuminated the beautiful. Like a child, I rehearsed his poetic line that tells an entire story again and again. I needed to confirm my own awakening. Dawn obliged, knowing that she is indeed the one I favor.

Soon after the greetings and the sharing of meals, Chet announced that another neighbor, John Schrock, would play guitar and sing. We met John when we first arrived in the valley. He stopped by one day when I was alone with my mother and introduced himself as a neighbor and a carpenter. In an unbelievable gesture of generosity, he offered his professional services to us at a neighborly half-price discount. He wanted us to feel welcomed. Both my mother and I liked him right away. My mother saw a depth of goodness in him, while I appreciated his youthful wit. After that first visit, John would occasionally stop by for reflective conversations—my favorite kind and apparently his too. We soon learned that John has a gentle, surrendering strength. He literally owns nothing and gives everything away, like the prophet you never met but always longed to know. And he is definitely different! With a ZZ-Top-like beard, an elastic conservative worldview, and a sinewy hold on Christianity, he walks the path of a spiritual pilgrim completely in thoughts, words, and actions. Imagine what Frances was to Assisi. Ever so slightly and perhaps only to me, John is to Belleville. Both mystics share the bizarre and the beautiful.

While we had discussed the meaning of life a few times with John, we hadn't had a chance to hear him play guitar. This neighborhood gathering introduced us to his music and, in turn, his soul. John writes prayerful songs that both inspire and provoke. With an enchanting, lucid baritone voice, he invites his audience to question and explore what they know and do not know about life. That night, John accurately intuited his audience and decided to play a few icebreakers that, by his own admission, "everybody should know." As he led, the neighborhood followed. Just as John assumed, they all knew the words. That is, everybody except me. Even Dawn knew some of the words. *Aha,* I thought. *They must be Protestant tunes!*

Catholics are rather finicky about their musical selections. Catholics tend to sing Catholic tunes arranged specifically for the mass, and perhaps more specifically, not for the Protestants. "Now, what do I do?" I mumbled at Dawn. Yes, folks were looking at me. As the schoolteacher, I knew I was expected to be singing. I thought, *Yes, I'm the one who lit the fireworks on a Sunday night, and my name does end in a vowel. Yes, I ate before the blessing. I am also the one Dawn favors. And, while we're at it, I don't have a vegetable garden. I can't quilt, and I don't can vegetables. But yes indeed, I can definitely fake it! I'll just pretend to sing, like Millie Vanilli, a referent that nobody else here is likely to know!*

For a handful of the more popular songs that I had never heard, I developed a quick knack for lip-synching. Still animated from my rock-n-roll days and, in a frantic effort to fit in, I did what was natural. I bobbed, swayed, and tapped my foot. That is until shamefully noticing that I was the only one even remotely in motion. No doubt, I'm the one who grooves to tunes and, good grief, I don't eat red meat either! Thank goodness for "This Little Light of Mine" and "Amazing Grace." These were two tunes I actually knew, so I sang them to high heaven. Grace saved me in more ways than one that night.

After a few icebreakers, John quieted the music and spoke openly to the crowd. With his tranquil, deep voice, he described a gift that he brought for me and Dawn. It was a bird's-eye view of the house. He and a pilot friend flew over Stonebridge the night before so John could take this picture, blow it up, frame it, and give it to us. It was a loving tribute from a gentleman we hardly knew yet strangely trusted. After John walked the photograph around the circle of guests, he returned to his guitar and introduced an original tune he composed just for the event—a gift of song written unexpectedly for Dawn and me. In it, John offered thanksgiving with a prayer. He beckoned the dreams in our new home to come true. I was deeply moved—entranced—that he could reach us with the language of his soul. Something unforeseen clicked. I cried on the inside. It was clear that my soul was receptive to his. I was turning outside in; a friendship that I hoped lasts forever was blooming.

Grace & Dawn

The pace is slow and friends are true,
Contentment is my hope for you.
Life is short, so do your best.

Chorus: Home sweet home is where the heart is,
And you've found yours.

Grace and Dawn have come in our midst,
And greeting you is on our list.
We give our hand and welcome you home.

Chorus: Home sweet home is where the heart is,
And you've found yours.

Fellowship is good and friends are kind;
The dreams in your heart I hope you will find.
May God bless you in all that you do.

Chorus: Home sweet home is where the heart is,
And you've found yours.

As I held onto the framed photo like a book of poems, John's song settled in our hearts. A few breathless moments later, Chet began setting paper bags filled with unwrapped gifts at our feet. I couldn't understand what was happening. I looked to Dawn for clarity, to see if maybe she could make sense of things. What are folks doing with these bags? Is this a custom that we're supposed to understand? All of a sudden, this awkward neighborhood gathering transformed into an amazing welcoming shower.

How can apparent strangers be so kind and giving? The two new gals who now live at Grace and Fran's place were visibly startled by these unexpected acts of love. The unbridled epiphany hushed us and moved us to tears with knees knocking. And with flustered cheeks, I suddenly understood why Chet implored us to be on time.

Welcoming showers apparently take place in the valley, although clearly, Dawn and I had no clue that such events even existed. Frankly, it's not something many city folks or suburbanites expect. In the valley, new neighbors can expect welcoming showers. To us, the mere concept was brand-new. Once again, what was frightfully amazing to us was simply familiar to nearby residents.

Each family honored us with their presence and welcomed us with food and useful gifts. Items like canned vegetables and jams, ketchup, cleanser, tissues, toilet paper, kitchen towels, trivets, and detergent filled the brown bags. Nothing was wrapped and everything was practical. Here we were—two women, two schoolteachers, two city gals, and two tremors of the earth who followed a calling to some house in the middle of nowhere—surrounded by beautiful strangers.

More than any other residual, it was clear that despite the blunders and bloopers, Dawn and I were blending in and belonging without even trying. Perhaps it's more accurate to say that Dawn and I were fitting an impression that was already there. We happen to be two women in Grace and Fran's house who fit their old patterns. People not only expected the wry irony of us, they embraced it. People not only expected the bizarre from us, they brought it out in us. Being like Grace and Fran, and being schoolteachers, anchored us home and rooted us as neighbor. All was as it should be.

Ordinarily two women would have to clear their own path to find warmth and welcoming especially, one would assume like I foolishly did, within an Amish/Mennonite farming community. But Grace and Fran had already etched that path and built that bridge for us, literally and symbolically. Grace and Fran already taught that lesson. They must have been wonderful teachers too, since their tales are still being told by protégés who listened. Theirs were tall shoes to fill. Little wonder then that my feet were getting cold, so I burrowed them into the grass to let the moment levitate.

Dawn and I walked home to get the car. We needed it to haul our gifts and to stabilize ourselves. By the time we returned to Chet and Julia's, our neighbors and budding friends had parted. This felt awkward and unsettling at first. We didn't get a chance to say thank you or even to say goodbye. It was a breach of cultural norms, especially for me. In my family's culture, departures are quite ornate and time-consuming. It usually takes forty-five minutes just to say goodbye. Not so around here apparently. Before returning home, I consciously made the effort to thank, with brevity, our hosts—the only folks remaining.

The compassion from neighbors lifted our hearts and kept us energized. We were forever moved by the generosity of those who would be considered strangers elsewhere but neighbors here. Neither of us could sleep. It was too late to call our mothers. Dawn and I talked through the night about every single detail. In some magical way, we were telling Grace and Fran all about it too.

CHAPTER 17

TRANSCEND WHERE YOU ARE

Do You Like Butter?

"I know we like butter,"
My sister told me.
"Sit down on this rock
Right now, and we'll see
If the buttercups know this
About you and me."

Then she pulled a bright posy
And, turning my head,
Held it under my chin
And laughed as she said,
"Your chin's yellow now
As the hair of your head."

Then I pulled a posy,
Held it to her chin,
And sure enough!
Yellow glowed brilliant again,
So that even her dimple
Shone deep in her chin.

August 6 had arrived. After straightening up, we loaded suitcases for our previously planned vacation to Cape Cod. There were lots of little things to do before leaving. Grace's memorial service was scheduled for midday. Since we would leave for the Cape afterward, we busied the morning with tidying and packing and then prepared for the service. Just as we were getting ready to dress, we heard an unexpected knock at the door that jolted us. Who could that possibly be?

Still in pajamas, we jumped. "You get it!" I insisted.

"No, you get it," Dawn retorted.

"I can't; I'm not dressed."

"Neither am I," she groaned with a sigh that sounded more like a whinny.

When it comes to dressing, Dawn has earned the Olympic gold. She can dress in lightning speed. So she sprinted to the door, gave the moment I needed, and called for me. Two unfamiliar guests entered the mudroom. They introduced themselves as Dennis and Judy Berman. Judy was Grace Straley's niece and the executor of her will. The Bermans had traveled from out of state to settle Grace's estate and to honor her last requests. Immediately upon hearing that she was related to Grace, I reached for her with a hug. A natural sense of kinship already bonded us. After welcoming them in, we watched the fascination in their eyes as they retrieved memories hidden in every corner of what they referred to as the "cottage." Apparently, it had been a while since they had been in their Aunt Grace's home. While Judy shared some nostalgia, I looked for traces of Grace in her expressions. She had to be in there somewhere. Seconds later, I spotted Grace nestled in the contours of her niece's smile.

Judy and Dennis had already heard about the two new women, the two schoolteachers—like Grace and Fran—who were living in the house. They wanted to learn how that could have possibly happened. How odd and yet, fitting? We briefly described how the house had called us to it, how it found us more than we found it—how we felt blessed to have met and connected with their Aunt Grace. They shared a few fun and favorite antics of their own and like light refracting from a jewel, their words glistened. Then Judy asked gingerly, "You wouldn't happen to be going to the service today, would you?"

"Yes, as a matter of fact, we do plan to attend, if that's okay," I hedged.

"I wondered," Judy replied with optimism. "We're glad you'll be able to come. Lunch will be served at the church hall afterward. Please feel free to join us."

With only slight hesitation, I said, "Thank you for the invitation. Let's see how things go. We have a long ride to Cape Cod ahead of us. We're leaving for vacation later today."

"Really?" Judy questioned curiously. "Cape Cod was where Aunt Grace and Fran used to go on vacation. They loved it there. That's why this home is the Cape Cod design it is!"

Dawn and I go to Provincetown, Cape Cod, if not every year, then every other year. P-Town gives elasticity to creativity. We were delighted to learn that Grace and Fran enjoyed the Cape too, although we're not sure if Provincetown was their special site. A few choice bulbous river rocks in the back patio though suggest it might have been— as does Grace's artwork and Franny's poetry. Provincetown has been a haven for literature and the arts for decades now. It is also a place where diverse experiences and expressions of love can be authentic.

The Bermans stared blankly into our faces as the odd coincidences between the aunts, this home, and the two new gals transfixed them a bit—they were also preparing for the memorial service for Grace. What happened next, after a slight lapse of time, was inexplicably predictable and unpreventable.

Judy meandered around a request with a courteous disclaimer. She might have even rehearsed it before saying, "We realize that different people have different views about this, and we respect the view that you have, but as you might have guessed, Aunt Grace was cremated." Then she paused to read our faces. "Depending on how you feel about this, we were hoping and wondering if you would mind if we spread Aunt Grace's ashes around the gardens here. It was what Aunt Grace wanted." Eternity whispered. I held my chest while holding back tears and assured her that "we would be honored. We hoped and prayed that Grace would come home. Apparently, Grace wished it too. Please relay our sympathies to your family and invite them back to your aunt's house after the service. They are all welcome to Grace's homecoming. She belongs here to rest."

Everything was as it should be or, as my mother would say, "As it was meant to be." The day we heard of Grace's passing, I wholeheartedly knew that her ashes would need to take root at Stonebridge. Her remains would be spread over the numerous and varied bulbs she once planted. The Bermans' request was more affirmation than astonishment. Grace would finally join the rocks, flowers, and trees that befriended her.

As we were leaving for the service and closing the door behind us, Dawn reached for my shoulder and emphasized, "Listen, if anybody asks us to speak in public, you do it, okay? You're the public speaker." I looked at her with a raised eyebrow and joked, "That's not likely to happen, is it? Why would it? Nobody knows us there." She rolled her eyes, suggesting, "Just in case, you wing it if asked." She smiled and raised her eyebrows back at me as we drove away.

To ready ourselves, we reflected on the passing of other loved ones as we approached the chapel. Dawn carried a bouquet of silver dollars with her to the service. Yet another remnant of Grace and Fran's gardens, silver dollars, also known as the money or honesty plant have a long, rich tradition in Dawn's matrilineal line. Her great-great-grandmother, great-grandmother, grandmother, and mother have all raised and sold silver dollars. The moment she saw the driveway lined with pedals of riches from an ancient tradition, Dawn's grandmother knew that this home was meant for her granddaughter. She and members of her family picked and peeled hundreds of them for use in dried flower arrangements. Once peeled, they look like small, translucent moons on golden shoots, each the size of a silver dollar. Perhaps Dawn's great-grandmother, who now bows proudly in the setting sun, used a royal carpet of honesty to welcome her great-granddaughter to Stonebridge.

While Dawn's ancestry presented themselves with the peel of a flower, mine made themselves known with the tick-tock of a kitchen clock. As I was hauling empty boxes down to the basement on June 28, our arrival day and the day of Grace's passing, I noticed a big, round, brass wall clock, designed like a pocket watch, sitting alone on the basement shelf. The clock was one I had seen many times before: "Oh, there's my grandmother's clock. I wonder who unpacked it." I looked around and found no clues as to how it got there. At first, I thought nothing of it, only that Dawn must have unpacked it for some reason and placed it on the shelf.

Later, I found the original clock of my grandmother's still packed in the box. An identical clock was sitting alone in the empty basement on a shelf. Otherwise, the shelves were barren. What are the odds? Granted, they're both old. Neither is worth much. But, because it's the clock from my grandmother's kitchen, it's priceless to me. Now there are two. That giant pocket watch brought me back to a kitchen where the loving wisdom of my mother's mother—a gifted, emboldened leader—transformed food into banquet and story into enchantment. Next to her kazoo and rosary, it's the only tangible treasure of my grandmother's that I have. Fortunately, infinite intangible treasures remain measures of ancestral love and can mean more than the passage of time—conversations, for example, like the one shared in the courtyard with Grace.

Dawn and I approached the chapel at Valley View Retirement Center with some trepidation. She checked her flowers. I checked my watch. We did not know what to expect. But we floundered our way in and found yet more bewilderment.

It was a spacious, simple room with chairs on either side of an aisle. In front stood a podium between two sets of naked windows. Noticing that the room was almost full, we hastened to secure a seat and opted to sit on the side with fewer people. After all, we were still strangers. I couldn't understand why all but one attendee was sitting on the right side of the room. Do people take sides at funerals like they do at weddings? I wasn't sure. It suddenly didn't matter. Dawn and I could not believe who the other lone star on the left side was. Could it be? How on earth is this possible?

"Jack! What are you doing here?" I blundered. "What are you doing here?" He reacted in kind, making it obvious that our befuddlement was mutual. Dawn and I were delighted to see him. First of all, it was Jack. Jack Troy, a colleague of mine, plain as day. Just by hanging out with him, people become more attuned to art and in turn, to life. Second, he must have known Grace and, with any luck, Franny too. If so, perhaps he would have Stonebridge stories of his own to share.

"Frances and Grace were friends of mine," Jack whispered. Then, with a more august tone, he leaned in to say, "I don't know if you know this, but Grace was cremated." He waited for our response. Dawn and I huddled nearer and nodded, "Yeah, we heard." "I offered to make the urn for her ashes," he continued. "It's there, on the altar."

Professor Troy has a soft-spoken, intimate, and piercing style. To many, he is an Einstein of pottery. A seasoned world traveler, Jack has that unique gift for living the art he loves. We felt relieved and proud to share this solemn occasion with him. With Jack sitting next to us, we now belonged.

During the service, various relatives and friends stepped up to the podium to relay favorite memories of Grace. We learned more about Grace's personality and pioneering spirit. Later, Jack approached the altar with a poem he wrote. In honoring Grace, Jack made certain to honor Frances too:

Above Front Mountain Road
(For Frances Barnes and Grace Straley)

Just before a trillion flakes shut out the morning light,
we gather at a kitchen window; watch the world
arrange itself for that demanding guest called winter.
Chickadees, juncos, titmice, rally their energized ounces
round the moss-backed cardinal. Her mate's brilliance
says resplendence thrives, even here, among inhibited hues.
But, as if not to dwell on the obvious,
your eye, Frances, spies dust on a jug's shoulder,
above a cupboard. My tiptoe grasp brings
one by one, teapot, mug, crock, jug after jug,
to the sink for a stern Protestant scrubbing.
Then, after cleanliness, comes poetry.

Fifty years of thumbing keeps Grace's book limber,
it's leather jacketing stanzas she knows by heart, or nearly so.
Frances squints for verses moored in memory;
they synchronize her rocking chair, her modulating voice.
Pinpoint us with a compass on the map.
How vast a circle might enclose three others reading and reciting
this December morning, cohorts in a secret scheme?
"Oh, read 'The Runaway.'
Have you ever heard such a picture of a little Morgan horse?"
We three outvote snow's tyranny,
gleaning the gist of memory's rootstock.
Though we must all go far from here, it won't be this morning,
from sunlight urging itself across a woven rug
like summer impinging on Big Valley.

It's grist for our gizzards, this poetry.
We keep remaking friendship fresh, and cardinal-bright;
besting the repertoire of wind, of season.
We'll grip in memory such a morning, our talons
fierce enough to ride a night-branch in a January storm.

Jack's eloquence celebrated Grace and Fran's passion for recitation and honored them appropriately, through poetry. After hearing about the January storm that Jack highlighted, I wondered if maybe he was the one who snapped that photo of Grace mounted in her room—the one of her sinking knee-deep while shoveling snow in their driveway.

Minutes after the ceremony ended, the pensive potter showed us the urn up close. This display of affection also gave us a glimpse into the love he held for the stone bridge builders. The urn shone with an earth-tone glaze, refracting the colorful memories Jack held. Afterward, we attended the luncheon at the community hall of Grace and Fran's old Presbyterian church. Jack sat next to us, exuding the gravity we needed.

While at the luncheon, just as Dawn intuited, we were introduced to an audience of around fifty and invited to give a little speech, to tell our own unfolding story of Stonebridge. I looked to Dawn for support, amazed at how she somehow knew to expect this, and poised myself. Relatives of Grace's seemed to study us with the hope of finding traces of the older spinsters. Or perhaps they sought to learn more about the spirit that carried their aunt into that setting sun.

After thanking Grace's family for welcoming us, I proceeded to tell them the story just as it occurred. With as much respect as possible, I stammered through:

> We feel blessed to be in the home that apparently meant the world to Grace and Fran. While we, unfortunately, didn't get the opportunity to meet Fran, we met Grace a few times and got to know her some. We've been getting to know them a lot better through the stories that neighbors and local residents share. They must have been quite a pair, the two of them—daring and dynamic.
>
> We can't help but believe that the house, their house, called us to it and that this valley called us here. A few months ago, I was scheduled to meet a friend for lunch. It was one of the first beautiful days of the spring season. So the restaurant filled with people wanting to greet the sun. I decided to sit outside to wait for my friend, but she was running late. To avoid the piercing gaze of hungry folks in line, I ran out to my car and grabbed an old newspaper from the recycling box stored in the trunk. While flipping through the pages, I noticed a small photograph of a home that was going to be sold at auction. I had never been to an auction before and didn't know much about them, but I knew that the description of the home was quite appealing. I showed Dawn the ad, and the two of us went to see the house that same day. It was truly love at first sight and then, sound. What do I mean? Well, Patty and George Knapp, whom some of you know, the folks who Grace and Fran sold the home to, shared the story of Grace

and Fran with us. We could hardly believe the amazing coincidences. Two schoolteachers—one, an artist and the other, a writer. One named Grace and the other Frances. Indeed, we're two schoolteachers. Dawn is quite an artist and, well, I'd like to consider myself a writer someday. We were wowed to learn that Grace and Fran built that bridge, planted those flowers, and left artwork and poetry behind. The night of the auction also happened to be, amazingly, Dawn's birthday. We won the auction that night and have been fascinated with the stream of serendipity that continues to flow. We feel thoroughly blessed to have been called to this home and valley. There have been so many synchronicities and moments of kismet that it would actually be more illogical not to believe than to believe. Little wonder then that we now call what happened, "a miracle." What's most startling is that our Amish and Mennonite neighbors all seem to expect two women, two schoolteachers, to live in that home too. Grace and Fran already pioneered that trail for us. People keep looking for resemblances. Well, theirs are big boots to fill, but we'll try to honor their memories with the respect they deserve.

Then, in an effort to share some of the limelight and embarrassment, I turned to Dawn to ask if she wanted to add anything. She simply said for all to hear, "No, you said it all!" I blushed and joined the laughter, still feeling humbled about dismissing the connection Dawn made back in April when she easily identified the glazed "Straley Barnes Arboretum" sign as Jack's. She was right all along. Meanwhile, the eccentric potter sat quietly at our table, chatting with Rae, a younger sister of Fran's.

I reminded the audience that they were invited to honor Grace's last wish by spreading her ashes around the property at Stonebridge, where Grace wanted to be. For the remainder of the lunch hour, cousins, nieces, nephews, and old friends approached one by one, curious to meet us. Many were enthusiastic to share memories with us, which was both humbling and baffling. We could not fully understand the attention. After all, we were strangers, weren't we? Yet we felt like family. It was as though we were the bridal couple in a receiving line. They were all so eager to introduce themselves to us, to shake our hands, to listen to our voices. They wanted to know who was who. Was I more like Fran and Dawn more like Grace, or vice versa? How do we echo their past? Might we share twin spirits?

Through my nervous, suburban lens, I attempted to lead the bereaved by announcing directions to their aunt's cottage. Fortunately, I caught myself only moments after drawing their attention. I quickly realized that a map wasn't necessary. In a valley without traffic lights, everybody already knew the way to Fran and Grace's. My newly formed audience was kind enough to allow the errant gesture go unnoticed.

The memorial procession of cars headed for Stonebridge. Of the fifty or so who were at the luncheon, approximately thirty returned to the house. Many parked in the driveway. Others parked along the street. A handful, led by Jack, gathered to walk the grounds where later they would, with reverence, scatter Grace's ashes.

Dawn and I opted to stay in the house to welcome the guests. Grace's sister, Bunt, captivated us. We could find Grace in Bunt's face, hear Grace in Bunt's style, and follow her in Bunt's stories. Through Bunt, we connected timelines and learned more about Fran and Grace. Dawn and I held onto morals about the Stonebridge gals like branches to trees.

A few relatives wanted to make sure that we had a cat, as Grace and Fran were known to have a few wild cat adventures. One of their felines, Eddy (named for education), was known to wander off. This worried Grace and Fran, so they concocted a device to keep him close by. They tied a long rope around his neck and attached a brick to the other end. This way, Eddy could only scurry so far. The memory prompted Grace's relatives to chuckle. Dawn wanted to assure the family that our kin-like fit was snug, so she gladly introduced our purring pet to them. "No, his name is not Eddy," she quipped with a playful sarcasm. "*Her* name is Whoa Nelly! Or Nelly Belly, Nell Belle, or Beelzebub!" They giggled again. Grace would have been pleased to see her impish spirit manifested this way.

In the meantime, Jack and his group returned for a soft drink. They appeared appropriately mystified by what they had just experienced.

Almost every niece and nephew—adults by now—asked if they could walk around the house for old time's sake. Dawn and I were delighted to discover that the house had carried that much joy for them. "Of course," we obliged. They continued to study us as though we had embodied the spirits of the couple who had walked this path before, looking more for a find than a fit. The fit was already there. Dawn and I mysteriously matched the archetypal imprint of Grace and Fran. A blueprint of their lives somehow replicated itself. Frankly, prior to this experience, we could not quite understand how the Dali Lama could be discovered. We now had a better appreciation for sacred serendipity, especially among strangers.

Like archaeologists of the spirit, Grace and Fran's relatives brushed gently the traces of ancient ruins in us. In a sense, Dawn and I were digging at the same site. They wanted not only to share and preserve memories; they might have wanted to liberate a few memories too. Together, we might mutually give birth to a cognitive elasticity that could free those of us who are kept bound by memories and those keeping memories bound. They saw the soul of an impish aunt inside an otherwise stranger and handed that stranger treasures of their aunt. In Dawn, and me, they saw their aunt who was single and who had connected creatively with another single woman for over sixty years. Perhaps they saw two unwed women, an artist and a writer, both schoolteachers who favor each other and both fitting. They might have been seizing an opportunity to understand our unique dyadic arrangement, especially if that opportunity was there before but had not awakened. Like Grace and Fran, maybe we had all become gardeners again, if only for the moment. In they who were strangers to us, we planted our trust. In we who were strangers to them, they planted their own transcendence.

During the service, Jack held on to a wild, fully fragrant orchid balanced delicately inside a hand-thrown vase. We assumed it was for a member of the family. As he prepared to leave, he offered the spiral, beige vase with flowers to Dawn and me, suggesting that, "It belongs here now with you. I didn't know exactly what I was going to do with it. Now that I'm here, back in this house, I'd like to leave it with the two of you." Jack hadn't realized that for years I had longed for a piece of his artwork. Cost or circumstance stood in the way. Dawn, who once studied pottery with Jack, was especially enamored with his kindness. Our hearts melted into that vase like the fire that glazed it. With precise timing, Jack was the first to depart. The rapport that was once collegial between us would become familial after this day.

Within the hour others approached, one by one, to bid us farewell. Each guest reached for us with long-lasting hugs, handshakes, or kisses. Some felt compelled to rummage through their wallets or pocketbooks for photos or mementos they had held on to for years. They wanted to give us something, to leave something behind perhaps in an effort to move forward. Anything ordinary suddenly appeared extraordinary by every stretch of the word. For some reason, relatives felt urged to not just show us but to give us things, like old photographs of Grace. Or they'd give possessions of Grace and Fran's and promptly demonstrate where they were once situated in the house. Dawn and I were deeply touched by their affections and generosity. We felt a little dazed as well.

After Grace's family departed, Judy and Dennis stayed behind to take in the day's vitality. In the meantime, Dawn and I walked the minister and celebrant of the service down our winding driveway. He also shared stories of his two parishioners Grace and Fran. We recalled the compassion he gave Grace that clear day we visited her in the gardens. At one point, he smiled, stepped back, and placed his hand up as though to hold me back. He felt momentarily daunted and uneasy that I "sounded so much like Fran that it was eerie." I smiled and accepted his comment as a compliment. Although I had never met Fran, the writer, I was delighted that others were finding her in me.

As the minister pulled away, we saw Judy and Dennis heading down the driveway getting ready to leave. Dawn and I hurried back so we could stroll with them. They emulated the warmth of the afternoon sun. After exchanging hugs, Judy offered us an old journal of Grace's

GRACE M. FALA, PHD

that chronicled her gardening escapades, the when and where of flowers planted in the arboretum out back. We gladly accepted. Then Judy looked at Dennis and turned toward us and said curiously, "Can you use a floor lamp?"

With eyes aglow, I immediately looked at Dawn and tapped myself on the head again. "Did you just say a floor lamp?" I asked Judy to repeat.

"Yes, we have this lamp from Aunt Grace's room. If you'd like it, you can have it."

"As a matter of fact, next to a ladder—that my mother just bought for us—it's the only thing we need. You really do have to watch what you wish for! Yeah, sure we'll take it."

They handed us the journal and a floor lamp, before hugging and bidding us farewell.

Dawn and I carried the keepsakes over the stone bridge and up the hill to the house. We were amazed that the only item of furniture we needed was a floor lamp, and it happened to be the item Grace left us after her final visit. We placed the lamp in the living room and sat down to study the photographs. There, in the center of a few pictures, was the same fixture in the same place. Grace apparently has a way of making light flicker—whether a setting sun or a standing lamp. We left for vacation, filling the tank with stories of gratitude and love.

CHAPTER 18

In Everything, Give Thanks

Ruby Throat

The ruby-throated hummingbird
Is quite the gallant lover.
His coat of iridescent green,
His red cravat, his brilliant sheen
Turn every head of every flower.
I saw him in a green glass bower
Of fragile touch-me-not.

With loving hum he kissed each one,
Each dainty orange flower.
Then whirring wheel in air he paused,
And jetted back with kiss to spare
From deep despair, a hiding one,
Pale faced, though fair.

Summer birds sing scat today. They thrill in sounds of Ella Fitzgerald and dance with the wind. I can hear their melodies from inside the rock sanctuary, where nature's music surrounds the arched doorway. Rocks can make the birdsongs sacred, as if hearing them for the first time. Little wonder that birds take flight. If I truly knew how to woo the universe much like the chickadee, flicker, finch, and hummingbird, I would fly too. Imagine the harmonic hum we could create simply by channeling the human heart into a jet stream of compassion. We could tap rhythms onto the breeze and clap messages across the universe. Imagine compassion. Or naturally, follow the swallows as they swoon and scoop up the sky with, and perhaps because of, divine providence. They're all on to something profound. I'm hoping that if I keep watching and listening closely, they'll be patient enough to share a secret or two with me, like they did with Ella. And like they and the flowers did with Grace and Fran.

Grace Viola Straley and Frances Martha Barnes knew and loved each other for over sixty years. They met during an era when seven counties in Pennsylvania integrated to form a "state normal school" for young women, mostly to study education. Later known as the State Teacher's College at Shippensburg, it is now Shippensburg University. Grace and Fran had just begun their brave professional journeys when they met.

Frances would later earn a bachelor's degree from the University of Pennsylvania and a master's degree from Northwestern University in Illinois. She was a teacher for thirty-five years. After instructing music at Manoa Elementary School, she taught English primarily to ninth-grade music classes at Haverford Township Junior High School located in Havertown, near Philadelphia. During her sojourn at Haverford, she also advised a popular, award-winning junior high school newspaper named *The Tattler.*

After retiring, Fran and Grace moved to the house they hatched and dared dream together from the mortar to the "Stonebridge." There, Fran could meld her talent for the pen with her passion for bird watching. Here, Fran wrote articles for the local newspaper inviting readers to *"Meet My Feathered Friends,"* that later became a compilation of writings detailing the flight and fancy of winged visitors. More of Fran's newspaper articles on nature are grouped together in *Have You Seen?* While Fran was engaging pen with paper, Grace would have been blending brush with paint. Or she was gardening.

Grace was an elementary school teacher for just as long. With a bachelor's degree from Penn State University and a master's degree from the University of Pennsylvania, she taught a variety of grade levels in the Lansdale school district, also a suburb of Philadelphia. While sharing professions as creative, dynamic educators, Grace and Fran lived together in the Haverford area of Philadelphia. Sometime before retiring, they designed the Cape Cod that they would someday build. They apparently fancied and fussed through every detail. Then they secured a prominent Philadelphia architect, Charles Okie, to draft the blueprints. The house was built to their specifications between 1962 and 1964.

Poetry, reading, music, and gardening were enjoyed by both residents and made Grace and Fran connoisseurs of conversation. Frances was known to be refined, dignified, and proper, as though she was teaching most of the time. She delighted in the recitation of poetry and often shared her writings with neighbors and friends. She had a warm and magnanimous personality. Townspeople often talk about how charismatic she was. And how she loved to cook and sing! Grace, who especially enjoyed Fran's culinary skills, was more down-to-earth and outdoorsy. Thinning the soles of rugged boots, Grace routinely gardened the nature trails and flowers in the back arboretum with poised persistence. She was also known for her ability to build things, design new things, and draw almost anything. When necessary, Grace could be stern yet witty. She also had a playful knack for storytelling, reminding listeners to "obey your instincts if they're right."

As they were getting ready to retire and as the house was being built, Grace and Fran spent their summers in the valley studying stonework. They specifically set out to break new ground by building the stone bridge that Dawn and I crossed the first day of our journey and have been crossing ever since. As Fran washed each boulder, Grace strategically cemented it into place. Impressed by this, we had to ask Grace about how she was able to engineer the hydraulics. She rumbled and smiled mischievously and winked, "We made it up as we went along." Grace and Fran were in their sixties when they built that bridge. By 1966, they were both retired and ready to move into Stonebridge, where they lived for close to thirty years before moving to Valley View Retirement Community.

Adults today remember days of their youth with Grace and Fran. In Big Valley style, folks prioritize the gardens first, the poetry second, and last but not least, the stories and games. They describe the attic upstairs as once being filled with pastime diversions and teachers' supplies. There were books everywhere too. To accentuate casual walks through the gardens, Grace and Fran would entertain their guests with the Latin names of indigenous trees and birds. They would invite friends to share a hearty recitation of poetry or a good board game. Children then remember clearly as adults now.

Apparently, Fran and Grace made a beautiful difference just by being themselves. They lived the nature, art, poetry, paradox, and play that they loved. Now they remain in the sweet fragrance of wildflowers. Anywhere we go in the valley and when we least expect it, townspeople go out of their way to tell a tale of the two unwed schoolteachers who lived in our house. Like a favorite song on repeated play, theirs is a song of civility that people enjoy singing. Folks speak admiringly of Grace and Frances when they see us, as if we were related. Like offspring, Dawn and I awaken memories that inspire joy. Folks remember Grace and Fran's arboretum, their stories, and their playful, influential personalities. Sometimes people stop by—out of the blue—just to visit the house, to meet the two new gals, to breathe in the spirit of wonder, and to reminisce. Not only can folks redeem the past, they transcend it too. Neither of us greets the other as stranger. Life, we have learned, can be fully experienced through the blessings of strangers. So each day, as we amble across the bridge or wrap ourselves inside this sanctuary of stones, a healing spirit beckons. Love is, after all, ageless, like the rocks.

Dawn and I drove over that bridge in our horse and carriage today. Our horse's tail waived high in the air and his hooves made a melodic clip-clop as we celebrated the sun's return to the season. The tasseled greens of the rolling cornfields glistened and swayed. The wheat whisked in rusted beige, and the surrounding trees dripped honey brown. It felt good to reflect the sun again and to appreciate its refining touch on nature.

As we toured the valley in our own "surrey with the fringe on top," we passed the usual handful of horses and buggies. One buggy in particular caught our attention. It was a black topper carrying a healthy young family. There were as many as five children huddled inside, dressed in their Sunday outfits. While her father manipulated the reins, his daughter delivered a cheerful wave that humbled us.

Where can city dwellers go nowadays to witness the honored traditions of an oral culture? Of a people who choose to remain close to nature and, fittingly, close to God? Where can folks shop on a tab with name only penciled on to the index card, pinned to a corkboard? Where else can you go to borrow a neighbor's horse? How often, anymore, can you buy pumpkins at a hut and leave payment in an open can?

Each of us is still very much on our shared journey. We have learned to listen to the languages of life and to heed the beauty and love of others. Meanwhile, the delicate Dutchman's breeches that carpet our arboretum are blooming. They add whimsy to the fantasies here. The soft-blue forget-me-nots already stand tall with their usual pride and conviction. They lean on the wind, winging bows for the butterfly applause. Grace and Fran's flowers still boldly proclaim their connections—like kin—to Mother Earth. Like kisses on the backbone of the valley.

Our names are on the roster of classes that each season teaches. Learning lessons from life and making it up as we go along, Dawn and I added a few chapters to the Stonebridge saga. With John Schrock as our friend, carpenter, and artist, we erected a four-stall, two-story barn in the frame that the Knapps cleared, precisely where my nephews and I lit the fireworks that first Sunday night, the Fourth of July. We also decided to build another bridge of sorts. With John Schrock again as the ideal mason, since he could blend creativity, engineering, and problem-solving into any project, we uprooted many of the indigenous rocks from the back patio and selectively placed them (after washing each one, of course, a la Grace and Fran) into what was intended to be a simple shed. But in time, the endeavor turned out to be less a shed and more a stone sanctuary—a bridge to the stars, perhaps?

While erecting it with John's assistance, we invited those we love to donate rocks from their favorite sites to the project. Each pebble or fossil they gifted would represent a special place, memory, and wish for us to plant in our rock recluse. The stones favored by those we love are now story keepers. Each one reminds us of particular family members and friends. Similarly, select stones from students and retreatants are fittingly mortared into our sanctuary. For example, in one corner of the room rests an original brick from Founders Hall of Juniata College. Students from clubs like AWOL and PRISM especially hail this sediment. Nearby it is a baseball-size piece of quartz from the SALE group at Shippensburg University. Our youth group, Agape, from the Kirkridge Retreat Center has some prominence in the center as a pomegranate-colored stone shaped like a heart.

Since being called to the valley, numerous members of youth groups and thousands of students from around the globe have visited Stonebridge. After crossing the bridge and while sitting in the shed-like sanctuary to engage and reflect, students are often encouraged to plant wishes like they would wildflowers. They are also welcomed to sing along with our feathered friends.

With each gathering, we share the story of Grace and Fran. Their narrative makes it easier for us to authenticate hospitality, to model what it's like for two teachers who identify as female to live and love together among the Amish and Mennonites. Their story exemplifies and, in some way, validates our teachings. Whatever the lesson, Frances and Grace's influence has been far-reaching and long-lasting.

Above the heavy, arched door are two wings of rocks, each embellished with gemstones. Dawn dipped choice gems into the one wing, and I smudged handpicked nuggets into the other.

What started with a stone bridge for dreams to awaken continues with a stone sanctuary for dreams to actualize. What started as a pebble prayer evolved into a mountain of miracles proving that, without doubt, even rocks have wings.

Directly above the entrance door to our mudroom, Grace and Fran's "shop" is a handmade shadowbox containing the two primary tools they used to build the bridge. Both tools are well-worn. The handle of the dimpled chisel hammer is patched with electrical tape, and the trowel that was once pointy and large is now smooth and small. Just below are Latin words imprinted in gold-leaf calligraphy that Grace etched. It reads "Pontem Fecimus," which translates to "We built the bridge."

"Cats" line drawing by Grace Straley

Grace's gold leaf of herself with Frances

Grace's painting of birds & flowers on kitchen wall

GRACE M. FALA, PHD

EPILOGUE

CELEBRATE SERENDIPITY

Amber in Fall

In the late light of autumn,
The willow leaves
Fall one by one
From the weeping trees.

Like beads of amber
From a broken thread,
Sunlight returns
To the fertile bed
Of all things wonderful:
Beauty, youth,
Age, wisdom,
Eternal truth.

One person in particular became an invaluable source of information and even more a treasured connection to our home and hearts. Dawn and I were especially blessed to maintain a friendship with a wonder woman, Rae, who we met at Grace's memorial service. Rae was Fran's younger sister, and through her, we were able to establish a sense of continuity. Rae was the third of five children and the only sibling still living when we entered the picture. Rae lived an active and full life on her own in a modest home in the heart of Belleville. Her husband, David Young, had died twenty-five years before her. She worked as a volunteer at the local fire company and was an active member of the local lodge. She also taught Sunday school at her church—the same place of worship that Fran and Grace attended. Like her older sister, Rae was a schoolteacher for close to thirty years. A 1933 education graduate of Juniata College, Rae invested most of her teaching years in the valley.

Early in her career, Rae taught all eight grades in a one-room schoolhouse in Belleville for five years. A potbelly wood burner was in the middle of the room and slate chalkboards covered every wall.

Students were blended then. Amish and English students studied in the same school. Later, Amish children started attending their own schools. Rae remembers having to stoke the fire to keep the classroom warm.

Her next move was to Somerset County, where she taught third and fourth grade jointly at Pretoria School for a year. After marrying David in 1937, her opportunities to teach waned. Married women were expected to be homemakers and were not encouraged to work outside the home. Persistent, Rae took a hiatus from teaching only for a short while. In 1942, because of the war, she was able to secure a one-year substitute position teaching all eight grades in another one-room schoolhouse at the Sample School just outside of Belleville. The next year a more marketable, unwed teacher was hired at Sample. Rae was not easily discouraged. In 1945, she was hired to teach first through third grades in Allensville, another neighboring town, where she taught for twenty-six more years until retiring in 1971.

Many generations have come and gone since Rae started teaching. Many remain in the valley. There isn't a person who knows this valley who does not know and respect Rae Young. For some, she has taught three generations of learners. Grandparents, parents, and children have studied their primary lessons with Mrs. Young. Amazingly and lovingly, Rae remembers most of the students she once taught. In fact, she has shown us a handwritten file she keeps in an old black marble composition notebook. In it, Rae updates the whereabouts and pivotal events of her former students. Tiny photographs of students as first graders are pasted next to information about when and where they married, how many children or grandchildren they have, where they work, and so forth. It is a cultural and historical marvel.

Mrs. Rae Young

Dawn and I became Rae's newest students. She taught us about the valley's best-kept secrets, the hidden floral trails, and community events. Because she garnered a lot of social attention and respect, Dawn and I became more popular when with Rae. We were honored to be in her company of friends.

Some days, however, I was neither student nor friend. At times, I felt more like a sister. We called each other just to check on things that didn't seem to matter much, but we did it anyway because the connection felt right. She once called to ask my advice, as a sister would, regarding a blurb she wrote for the church bulletin. I called her back to ask her about the chicken corn soup at the festival and when it would be served.

Once, when Dawn and I visited Rae to appreciate the fresh, delicious homemade cookies she baked, she inadvertently called me Fran. Realizing her mistake, she said that I was a lot like Fran, even though my name is Grace, but that Dawn was like Fran, too. Yet she was convinced that we both had a little of Grace in us as well. She looked earnestly at us in an effort to capture the wonder of it all. Rae helped us to feel connected. When she returned to Stonebridge for a visit, she too felt at home. Not surprisingly, Fran's kid sister knew the flowers in the backyard by their fragrance too. Mrs. Rae Young lived her ninety-four years fully. Miraculously, her funeral happened to be on a snow day, so we "gals" could attend without hassle.

Nowadays, we look for her teacher's touch, that penciled swoosh in the setting sun, as one among many that Stonebridge has given us. Rae rests nearby her sister, alongside the mountain laurel and redbud trees. Rocks from her garden also settle with stillness in the sanctuary into these weird yet wondrous, winged walls.

Frances Barnes, Rae Young & Grace Straley

Dawn and Grace

"We Built the Bridge"